Four Generations

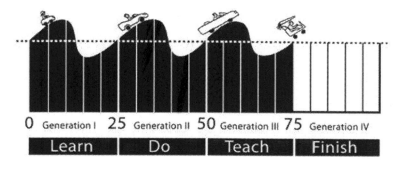

A Journey Through Life

"From Grandpa With Love"

Christmas 2017

Wishing You a Blessed Christmas!

Marvin and Joan Martin

A Collection of Later in Life Writings
"From Grandpa With Love"

…for I, the Lord your God, am a jealous God,
punishing the children for the sin of the fathers
to the third and fourth generation of those who hate me,
but showing love to a thousand generations
of those who love me and keep my commandments.
(Exodus 20: 5a-6; Deuteronomy 5:9a-10)

A Personal Note

I pray that you find *Four Generations: A Journey Through Life,* (including my *World War II Diary*) an enriching and profitable experience.

This is the first in a series of five books *"From Grandpa With Love"* consolidating booklets I have written over the past 35 years to pass on what God was teaching me about life. The material has been available on the internet at *fromgrandpawithlove.com,,* but printed books have been suggested. So, God willing, the following additional books will gradually be completed and available through Amazon and local book stores by the time I reach age 90 next year:

Faith

Marriage

Vocation

Passing It On

I thank all those who have contributed so graciously and generously to me in countless ways during my "journey." Without you, this material would never have been born!

God Bless You All.

Marvin J. Martin
Wichita, Kansas, 2014

DEDICATION

*To our children, grandchildren, and great grandchildren,
together with all the family of God
He has so graciously brought into our lives.*

ISBN: 1497503760
ISBN 13: 9781497503762
Library of Congress Control Number: 2014906238
CreateSpace Independent Publishing Platform
North Charleston, South Carolina

CONTENTS

WELCOME TO
FOUR GENERATIONS:
A JOURNEY THROUGH LIFE.

Hopefully reading this book will be an enriching and up-building experience as you reflect on your life's journey to date, note where you and your loved ones are now, and seek to determine where and how God wants to use you during the years ahead. 3500 years ago, Moses wrote:

> *The length of our days is seventy years—or eighty, if we have the strength; yet their span is but trouble and sorrow, for they quickly pass, and we fly away... Teach us to number our days aright, that we may gain a heart of wisdom.*
> (Psalm 90:10, 12)

This is still good advice. Life expectancy for a man today is about 80 years. That's approximately 29,000 days. At my age of 88, I am living on borrowed time. I am deeply aware how important it is for us all to "number our days aright"!

People have asked how this material came to be compiled. It all started about 20 years ago. As I approached age 70, I decided it was time to look back and prepare a family genealogy to pass on to my children and grandchildren. After working on the project awhile, it became apparent that I was acting as a reporter to discover and pass on third-hand information about people I did not know and events I had not witnessed; and that my children and grandchildren did not yet really know me. I determined, therefore, to first prepare and pass on to them an eyewitness account of my own 70-year span of our family history.

As I attempted to set forth my life journey on paper, I struggled to find a Biblical pattern to follow. The Bible often speaks of "generations," particularly to the "third and fourth generation" (e.g., Exodus 20:5–6; 34:6–7). But it seemed there were two ways to view these generations.

First, was the normal view of a Great-grandfather, Grandfather, Father and Son. Using a life span of 75 years and generations of 25 years each, four generations span about 150 years. For example:

> In 1900- Great-grandfather is born.
> In 1925- Grandfather is born.
> In 1950- Father is born.
> In 1975- Son is born.
> In 2050- Son dies.

This view is important, and we will spend some time discussing it as we go through our material.

But the *second* view, and the one that particularly caught my attention, was the realization that *each of us who live an 80-year life-span actually live in four generations in our own lifetime!* And we often do it in segments of about 25 years each. The first three generations seem to follow the pattern of Ezra 7:10 (study, do, and then teach) and to be followed by a fourth generation in which we finish our race. When viewed this way, the concept began to look like this:

Generation I	0–25 years	Child	"Learn"
Generation II	25–50 years	Parent	"Do"

| Generation III | 50–75 years | Grandparent | "Teach" |
| Generation IV | 75–onward | Great-grandparent | "Finish" |

Someone has referred to our four periods of life as "Spills," "Thrills," "Bills," and "Pills!"

When I looked at each 25-year generation of my life, I found there also appeared to be five subchapters of about five years each. Undoubtedly these divisions are somewhat arbitrary, and the actual timing and sequence will vary from person to person. But after reviewing lives in the Bible and looking at my own life and the lives of others, I found an amazing similarity in the paths many of us seem to follow through life.

It's as if we are all on a common journey, and—as a result— many of us seem to have somewhat predictable experiences at somewhat predictable periods of our lives. Once that pattern becomes apparent, we begin to see a rhythm in our own lives and in history that can be helpful as we chart our life journeys and watch the journeys of those around us.

After reflecting on the effect of charting my own life, I realized that I needed to share the concept with others. Therefore, I began to meet with groups of men (and later, groups of men and women) of all ages to go through this information and discuss it together. While we found there were many differences in our journeys, we also found there were often many amazing similarities.

The material has matured a great deal since that first meeting. I have learned so much from so many. About five years after the original information was sent to our family, I wrote this book covering up to Age 75. At that time, I committed to our family—and others who were interested—that I would try and write about each new 5-year period, as I completed, or neared the completion of those segments.

I added "Onward and Upward" (Age 75-80) in 2005, and "Letting Go" (Age 80-85) in 2010, which brings us to the end—at least for now.

As you read, please keep the following in mind:

1. These are my impressions. Hopefully my journey will serve as a grid and give you some examples. But life is not the same for everyone, and you will have to make your own decisions regarding what will and will not apply to you.

2. The material is short, basic, and comes from my own unique experiences. You will need to utilize your own experiences and research and determine how you want to proceed with your life, just as I have decided for my life.

3. The writings occur at various times, so my comments at one point may not always reflect what I came to understand and write later in life.

4. You need to test the material against the scriptures and the counsel of Godly people in your life, and then hold on to what is good and discard what is not (1 Thessalonians. 5:21–22).

Two extra tools are offered to help you as you chart your life journey:

> *First* is a "Life Line" at the end of the book that sets out the general structure I have adopted for my life and that you may want to consider for yours.

> *Second* are the questions at the end of each chapter that you may wish to ponder and answer. These questions have all been important in my search. I do not believe that you have to wait as long as I did to answer them. Dealing with these issues earlier in life may enhance, and perhaps change, the course of your journey.

Let me close this introduction with one final observation. For several years, I have been concerned that we are increasingly living in "Age Ghettos" where we often draw into our own age groups for comfort and community. While identifying with those who are in the same life stage is necessary and good, I hope this study will allow us to strengthen community across the whole spectrum of life.

For those who are young, may it give hope and direction for the future; for those in the middle years, may it give an opportunity to regroup and make straight your course for the future as you lead those following you and look forward to models up ahead; and for those in the later years, may you see what a marvelous opportunity you have to pass on what you have learned to those who are following and often desperately looking for "The Way."

And now may our Lord enlighten and encourage you as you listen and walk out the rest of your life in dependence upon Him, His Word and His Spirit, aided by the counsel and direction of those whom He has called to that purpose for you.

From Grandpa with Love

Generation I:
A Time to Learn
Age 0–25

Train a child in the way he should go,
and when he is old he will not turn from it.
(Proverbs 22:6)

These are the preparation years, the "springtime" of our lives, when we are each a "child" struggling to become an adult. These are years that can deeply influence and affect all the rest of our lives and the lives of those who follow us.

THE GIVENS
AGE 0–7

From one man he made every nation of men,
that they should inhabit the whole earth;
and he determined the times set for them
and the exact places where they should live.
(Acts 17:26)

We all enter life at a certain time and place that we do not control. We have nothing to do with when we are born, where we are born, or to whom we are born. We do not choose our gender, race, color, or ethnic background; neither do we choose our ancestors' reputations or economic statuses. We do not choose our early models, good or bad. Neither do we have any control over our early training or discipline, or our lack of them. We do not have anything to do with the mind, body, or emotions we receive at birth. These are all "givens" in our lives.

Sometimes we are prone to speak of someone who rises to prominence out of obscurity, or through difficult beginnings, as a "self-made" person. But when we look deeply, we usually find inherent qualities that—while laudably honed and strengthened by the individual—were often based on a set of givens over which we had no control.

God Made Us Perfect
I am becoming increasingly convinced that God creates us all perfect for the roles he has designed for us to carry out during our time here on earth. Our job is not to be self-made, nor to make ourselves over to become what we want to be, but rather

to surrender ourselves to God and embrace what He has created us to be. Until we recognize and accept our givens, it will be difficult for us to reach the potential and fulfillment God has designed for us.

Once we eliminate personal responsibility or credit for the givens in our own lives, we eliminate much of the source of envy, ingratitude, and even anger that may spring from feeling that we were victims who were born inferior. In the same way, a realistic acknowledgment of our givens can also help us strike down much of the unjustified pride and arrogance that can mistakenly arise from being born with exceptional physical or mental capabilities or wealth, prestige, heritage, or tradition.

But We Got Contaminated
Although God may have created us perfectly to carry out his purposes, we must keep in mind that there is sin in the world (and has been since the time of Adam and Eve). We are warned in the Ten Commandments that God punishes the children *for the sin of the fathers to the third and fourth generation* but also promises that He will show *love to a thousand generations of those who love me and keep my commandments* (Exodus 20:5–6; see also Exodus 34:6–7).

We are, therefore, a mixture of blessing and burden. We are blessed by what God created for good and by our ancestors' obedience and love for him but, sadly, we are also burdened with the sin of Adam and the unique sins of past generations, which have contaminated and confused God's perfect creation.

Biblical Examples

Let's look at two of the many Biblical examples of these family punishments and blessings promised in Exodus 20:5–6 and 34:6–7.

1. *The Patriarchs* (Genesis 20–50) As Charles Swindoll has discussed in his excellent tape, *Breaking Granddad's Bent,* a family sin of lying passed from Abraham down to his son, Isaac, and then on to his grandson, Jacob. Grief and punishments followed these lies down through three generations. This family bent continued to the fourth generation as Jacob's children sold their brother Joseph into slavery and then lied to their father and led him to believe that wild animals had killed Joseph. Fortunately, that was not the end of the story. Joseph, by steadfast devotion and obedience to God, broke the family bent and recovered the blessings for himself and the generations who followed!

2. *Leah* (Genesis 29–30) Follow also the exciting story of the life of unloved Leah in Genesis 29-30, and see the great blessings that flowed to her and her descendants because of her faithfulness to God. Leah was married by the deceitfulness of her father, Laban, to a man (Jacob) who did not love her. She was forced to live out her life in the shadow of her younger and more beautiful sister, Rachel, who was Jacob's other wife and true love. Yet, Leah remained faithful to God and to her marriage. As a result,

When the Lord saw that Leah was not loved, he opened her womb,
(Genesis 29:31)

and gave her six sons, including Judah and Levi. Four hundred years later, Leah had become the "mother" of over one million descendants, including Moses and Aaron! (See Numbers 1.) And for real excitement, read the genealogy of Jesus in Matthew 1 and Luke 3, and realize that this unwanted and unloved woman of God was also the "mother" of all the priests, and all the kings from David down to the Lord Jesus!

It is clear that our faithfulness and our unfaithfulness do matter—not only for us but also for generations to come!

Modern Day Examples

For more current examples, you might look at two books about the families of three twentieth-century presidents:

1. *The Roosevelt's: An American Saga* This book by Peter Collier contrasts the family of President Theodore "Teddy" Roosevelt with the family of President Franklin D. Roosevelt and his wife, Eleanor (who was the daughter of Teddy Roosevelt's brother). It is almost impossible not to see both the strengths and weaknesses that characterized the descendants of each of these men and their wives for generations.

2. *The Sins of the Father: Joseph P. Kennedy and the Dynasty He Founded* In his book Ronald Kessler describes the family background of President John F. Kennedy and shows how family traits flowed down through the generations.

Sorting Out Our Family Traits

We need, therefore, to study the givens that have been passed down to us and to sort out the good heritage from the bad.

We need to eliminate the bad bents we have inherited. We also need to hold on to and magnify the blessings that have come to us from prior generations. And the good news is that we can do both of these things if we will repent, place our trust in Jesus, and allow His Spirit to indwell and direct our lives.

Remember, too, that we are probably all prejudiced in our thinking and analysis because of our givens and experiences in life. As one speaker put it, "We give an unbiased account of the Civil War, from the Southern (or Northern) point of view!" Just as we need to break the harmful bents in our own lives, we also need to realize and deal with similar bents in the lives and conclusions of others—including mine as expressed in this book. We must always test against the Holy Scriptures to determine what is really right and true. As Paul warns in his letter to the church of the Thessalonians,

> *Test everything. Hold on to the good. Avoid every kind of evil.*
> (1 Thessalonians. 5:21–22)

This is a lifetime task, and we will probably never fully succeed. But it seems the place to begin is to list, and then start to deal with, each of our own unique givens. As one example of givens, and in order that you might better understand and evaluate the comments and conclusions expressed in this book, I have listed below some of my givens as I see them. Later, you will have the opportunity to list and then determine some of the effects of the givens that you have received from God as passed down to you from prior generations in your family.

Some of My "Givens"

1. Personal
   - Born in 1925, in Wichita, Kansas—that placed me in the Great Depression and the World War II generation in the heartland of the most powerful and affluent nation the world has ever known.
   - Male, growing up with two older brothers.
   - Word-worker, but little talent for physical work.
   - White, Anglo-Saxon, Protestant (WASP), so unable to feel, firsthand, the problems, pain, and difficulty of minority status.
   - Healthy mind and body, but not prone to the challenges of illness.

2. Parents
   Marriage
   - Committed relationship for thirty-three years until my father's death.
   - Father was solid male image and strict disciplinarian.
   - Mother was a feminine role model, supporter of her husband, and nurturer of her children. Family life was a high priority.

   Faith
   - Loyal baptized church members. Attended Sunday morning services regularly, but little other involvement in church life or structure during my lifetime.
   - No direct involvement in public charity. Faith was a private matter.

Occupation
- Father had an eighth-grade education and worked as a farmer, stockman, merchant, and funeral director in his earlier years. Always an entrepreneur, he later became a custom homebuilder.
- Mother had to quit school in the tenth grade to work and became a bookkeeper. During their marriage, she was a dedicated wife and mother. After Father's death, she managed several apartment buildings for over twenty-five years until her death.
- For both parents, self-reliance was a high priority. Father encouraged me, "Never work for anyone else." Individualism, more than team effort, was modeled.

Community
- Loyal citizens, but no governmental service or political advocacy. Three sons' decisions to enter flight training in World War II were supported.

- Deep concern over government's increasing role in financially supporting and controlling lives of citizens. Believed that government should not stifle individual effort or responsibility.

Privacy
- Personal and family matters were handled privately.

3. Grandparents
- Sadly, I know very little about my grandparents. I have no personal recollection of seeing any of them except on one

(or was it two?) brief visit(s) with my aged paternal grandmother shortly before her death. Over the years, I received some secondhand information about my maternal grandfather (a pastor) and grandmother (a homemaker) from family stories, pictures, and sermon notes. But I had virtually no information about my paternal grandparents except names, places of residence, and occupations. (Grandfather was a farmer, and Grandmother was a homemaker.) Later one of my nieces, who was working on our family genealogy, sent me a lengthy obituary she had discovered that opened up a whole new world for me. For the first time, these older ancestors from whom I had descended began to be a reality and part of my history, and I am deeply grateful!

4. Great-grandparents
- Now that the door is opened through this new information, I am learning at least a little about the families and histories of some of my great-grandparents and about whom I have known so little for so long.

As I think about these bygone people, it is strange to realize I have received both good and bad from earlier generations, so many of whom I did not even know. While it makes the task more difficult, it does not relieve me of measuring my life against God's Word, and asking Him to work through me to overcome the sins and pass on the good to those who follow me.

Now we come to our first questions.

QUESTIONS

1. What are your "Givens"?

2. Identify and list your healthy "Family Bents."

3. Now identify and list your unhealthy "Family Bents."

4. How can you correct the unhealthy "Family Bents" and encourage the healthy ones for those who follow you?

CHILDHOOD
AGE 7–12

Children, obey your parents in the Lord, for this is right.
"Honor your father and mother"—
which is the first commandment with a promise—
"that it may go well with you and that you
may enjoy long life on the earth."
(Ephesians 6:1-3)

Over a generation ago, my wife and I sat one evening in the living room of our pastor's home. We were about to embark on our first small-group experience with a few other couples from the small church we were attending. The pastor opened the discussion by saying he wanted us to answer a series of questions designed to break down barriers and begin to establish real fellowship with one another. The questions, he said, were called the "Quaker Questions," I suppose because they originated from some members of that Christian denomination.

"Think back to ages 7 to 12", he directed, "and tell us *first* where you lived, *second* how you heated your homes, and *third* what the warmest (most memorable) room in your home was." Hours later we had begun to bond together and build relationships by opening the doors for one another to some of our most poignant childhood memories.

Ages 7 to 12 seem, uniquely, to be years when we establish deep, lifetime memories. These years are often the golden age of our childhood. And so it was for me. It was during these years that I formed much of my belief system. These early experiences, together with the "Givens" we discussed in the last chapter, helped to develop in me deeply engrained views of right and wrong, life and death.

Home

The real estate business collapsed due to the Great Depression. In 1932, at age 7, I moved with my family to a ten-acre tract north of Wichita that we always called simply, "The Farm." It had a big, old two-story farmhouse, a barn, a windmill, and outbuildings. With hard economic times, dust storms, and farm living, it was probably a difficult time for my parents. But this farm playground with a horse, a dog, a river, and a close family made it a boyhood dream for me. I realize my lifelong sense of family solidarity and security was built during these early years.

Work and Pay

Milking cows, cleaning out manure, raising and killing chickens, and tending a vegetable garden all provided an early work ethic. There was no opportunity (and probably no time) for organized athletics. Although I never realized it then, our lives were being trained toward productivity and service rather than toward the competition that is so prevalent in almost every part of our adolescent and adult culture today. There was, however, boyhood bickering and sibling rivalry—a deeply engrained desire to be different and to excel in my own area of endeavor rather than following the lead of an older brother. The blessing and curse of "individualism"!

My pay allowance was twenty-five cents a week from which I was to "save some, spend some, and give some." It really wasn't so bad because twenty-five cents would buy two hamburgers (five cents each), a "coke" (five cents) and a Saturday Movie Matinee (ten cents). From the beginning, my father taught us to work, to become self-reliant, and to expect to be on our own by age 18. As training, he gave me a calf to raise and care for and agreed to buy it back for twenty-five dollars when it was grown. Owning a bicycle—and later an automobile—was permissible, as long as we earned the money for them. Things I worked to obtain always seemed to have more value.

School

A small, two-room country school (with grades one through four in one room and grades five through eight in the other) provided an opportunity to interact with various ages and academic levels as the classes worked and recited openly one-by-one during each day. I have since realized it isn't beautiful school buildings but dedicated parents and teachers who help build students.

Vows

Kansas was a "dry" state where alcoholic beverages were illegal. Representatives of the WCTU (Women's Christian Temperance Union) came to our school, condemning the evils of alcohol. I took the pledge never to use it. Many years later I had to come to grips with this and other vows I had made. I found it to be a far-reaching experience, as I first contemplated the seriousness of vows and God's admonition:

It is better not to vow than to make a vow and not fulfill it.
(Ecclesiastes. 5:5)

and then sought to comply with my promises.

Discipline

Discipline was tough at home and at school, but it worked. Being "shaken until your teeth rattled" by my fourth-grade teacher brought deep respect and a relationship that lasted into adulthood. We weren't spanked often at home but, when it happened, we didn't forget. The last time Dad spanked me was with a razor strap. He spanked my two brothers and me for stealing some of his green Mexican cigarettes and then lying to him and saying we hadn't taken them. The cigarettes were awful. So was the whipping. But again, it was deserved. I do not ever recall any rancor or bitterness over my parents' discipline or treatment of me. I never doubted their love and concern for my welfare. And I never had any doubt that stealing was wrong and that lying only compounded the problem!

Vacations

I also learned the value of family vacations. Memories of the car trips, tents, and cabins, the views we saw, and the adventures we shared as a family are still vivid over 60 years later.

Life and Death

It was during these years that I began to see the reality of life and death. As the animals bred and then delivered their young, we learned about sex at a young age. When male ("Tom") cats came back and deliberately destroyed the young litters they had fathered, we learned there was a key difference between animals and people. And as animals died and were buried or were hauled off to the desiccating plant with their stiff legs pointing up out of the open truck, we learned the physical side of death.

During this time I also had my own first personal encounter with death. One of our young group members at a summer camp drowned in the river swimming area, and several others—including me—almost drowned. I still recall looking up and seeing a cloud and wondering if it was the last cloud I would ever see, and then hearing a voice call out from the bank, "Swim with the current." Later I listened intently as an observer recounted how the young lifeguard, who had become my boyhood idol, courageously saved some boys and almost lost his life in the process. The next few days we heard them set off explosives trying to raise the drowned boy's body. The episode climaxed with us all attending his funeral. This experience gave me a new sense of my own mortality and provided a myriad of lessons about life, death, and courage that I have pondered and used many times during later years.

God and Church
It was during these early years that I first heard God—not verbally, but in the sense of having a growing assurance that He wanted to be present in my life and that I needed to move closer toward Him. I was baptized (it was cold), and I tried repeatedly to read through the Bible but stumbled over King James language and Old Testament concepts. I prayed at night, so I presume my parents taught me. We had a standard mealtime prayer, a church relationship, and we occasionally sang hymns around our piano at home. But I had no Bible studies, youth groups, or Christian fellowship to help me into a personal, loving relationship with Jesus. I now see how valuable these can be. Would they have been enough to bring me closer to Him at an earlier age? I honestly don't know, but I believe it would surely have been worth trying.

Conclusion

These then are some of my age 7 to 12 memories. I've purposely set them out in detail to show how deeply these early memories have affected my values and actions all through my life. I expect your early memories will be equally important for you. As I look at today's fragmented society and it's broken marriage relationships, I am painfully aware of the great debt I owe to my parents: for the security of a father who provided for us and gave us strong leadership and discipline, and for a mother who stayed close by to feed and clothe us, nurse us when we were sick, and comfort us when our world fell apart.

Let me add a word of caution here. Memories get distorted over the years. Some time ago my older brother and I were nostalgically reminiscing with our wives about earlier days. As the morning wore on we found ourselves with differing recollections of the same events. "Do you remember how we...?" one would say, and the other would reply, "Well, I remember, but I think we..."

"No, no" was the response, and off we would go trying to convince each other that our version was correct. Finally our two wives walked out of the room, and one said to the other, "I don't think they grew up together!"

But whether right or wrong, these are our perceptions and memories of what took place. These memories, together with our givens, are the foundation upon which much of the rest of our lives are built. Where they are faulty and weak, I pray we will recognize and set about to discontinue the bad; and where they are strong, I pray that we will hold on to—and magnify—the good so that we can bless those who follow us.

Now it's time to turn the journey back to you and let you consider some questions about this important chapter of your life.

QUESTIONS

1. What are some of your strongest childhood memories? (Feel free to refer back to the categories in this chapter, if you need a springboard for your memories.)

2. Which childhood memories have most affected your life, and how?

3. Consider how these memories—both good and bad—could benefit people in your sphere of influence.

4. How can you pass on these memories to those who follow you?

THE TEENS
AGE 12–18

*Remember your Creator in the days of your youth, before the
days of trouble come and the years approach when you will say,
"I find no pleasure in them..."*
(Ecclesiastes 12:1)

A Time for Choices

These are the years when we usually begin to make major choices
on our own. If we have had good givens and memories from
our ancestors and early years, our choices during our teens
will hopefully be good ones. If our earlier years have not been
positive, we may make choices that will adversely affect us, those
around us, and those who follow us. Fortunately, as we will discuss
below, Jesus gives us the opportunity to correct our course and
to follow Him.

Even with proper background and training, the teenage years
are usually accompanied by such increased freedom that some
problems are almost inevitable. The Bible notes:

> *Train a child in the way he should go,
> and **when he is old** he will not turn from it.*
> (Proverbs 22:6, emphasis added)

This seems to leave open, or even underscore, the fact that
there is a tendency for each of us to rebel and stray during
these youthful years. There appears to be at least a little of
the Prodigal Son (Luke 15) in us all. Perhaps that's why Paul
warns his young friend, Timothy, to "flee the evil desires of

youth…" (2 Tim. 2:22). Paul also gives his protégé, Titus, only one encouragement for young men in Titus 2:6 (i.e., "to be self controlled").

The Most Important Choice

As I have grown older, I find younger people increasingly asking me, "What would you do differently if you could live your life over again?" In other words, "What choices would you make differently?" (I think I would like it better if they would ask me what I did that was right; it's always more uplifting to discuss our successes!)

In considering this question, I have concluded that there is one decision that dwarfs all the rest. It is a choice that I did not make until my mid-forties. It is the choice we have prayed that our children will make, and that we now pray almost daily for our grandchildren and great grandchildren: that they would follow, love, obey, walk with, and serve Jesus as the *Lord* of their lives. My great regret is that I did not make a *Lordship* decision for Jesus early in my life, at least by my teenage years, rather than fighting Him for years and attempting to live both in the ways of the world and also to follow Him. I believe this one choice—whether I am going to *surrender* to God, or to try and run my own life—affects all the rest of my life, both in this world and throughout eternity. I realize now that this decision also has major ramifications for all those around me and for those who will follow me down through the generations. I think the lasting consequences of this choice will probably be true for you, too, and for all those who are in your sphere of influence and following you.

Charting Our Life Lines

The teenage years begin at almost the exact middle of Generation I. As I look back on my own youth—and later observed our children and now our grandchildren—I have concluded this is a period in life when we see childhood receding and adulthood approaching with all its opportunities, but it is also a time full of challenges and responsibilities. We feel ourselves changing physically, emotionally, mentally, and spiritually, and we are both exhilarated and frightened. We intuitively seem to realize we need to make great changes during the next few years to prepare us for Generation II (Age 25-50) and beyond, but we don't really know precisely what to do. In addition, most young people seem to have a very short sense of time. Six months is a long time when you are 15 or 16! As a result, teens may think and act in ways that give them short-term rushes without considering that they may result in a lifetime or an eternity of pain and regret. The devil often seems to offer immediate pleasure, but long-term hangovers.

The encouraging note is that everyone must go through these years. I believe the "Traumatic Teens" are simply the first in a series of three rapids most of us encounter as we travel down this river of life. Later we often go through a mid-life crisis and the "Funky Forties" as we prepare to leave Generation II, at about age 50. And still later we will likely encounter a similar period of unrest as we move out of the work place and walk through the "Sober Sixties".

Thus, when we chart our own life journey along our "Lifelines", we often see a rollercoaster pattern begin to emerge. The first half of each generation period usually seems upbeat, sometimes almost euphoric. For example, what is a better time of life for most of us than the wonderful childhood years up to age 12? But suddenly puberty and youthful freedom spin many of us toward the rocks, and we struggle to correct our courses and work through the "Traumatic Teens". In view of this pattern, the first part of our life often looks like this:

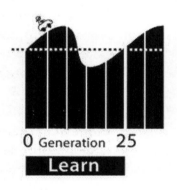 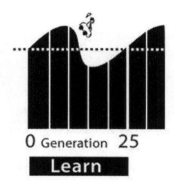

A Time to "Convert"

At each of these turbulent, and often troublesome, times we frequently take stock of our lives and—after much railing and suffering—we chart a course for the years ahead. These are times when we are inclined to convert to something as the passion of our life. For some teenagers it may be sports, for others academic achievement, or girls, or alcohol, or fame, or cars—or Jesus Christ! At stake is the ageless choice of whether we surrender ourselves and use the three great blessings of Pleasure (including sex), Possessions (including money) and Power (including fame and position) for the glory of God and the benefit of others—or whether we embezzle them and use them for ourselves.

Recognizing Our Era

I believe the era in which we live affects our choices greatly. I was 14 when Hitler invaded Poland in September 1939. Hearing thousands of Germans fanatically chanting "Sieg Heil" over the shortwave radio as they thundered their allegiance to Adolf Hitler chilled me. I was 16 when Japan bombed Pearl Harbor on December 7, 1941. These World War II events eclipsed everything else. Along with all my friends and family, I seemed to think and talk constantly about "The War". As I prepared myself to enter the military service, the war increasingly became my motivation and my passion during these teen years.

I have come to believe that our era is the cultural climate and activities that were in effect during the first 25 years of our lives—particularly during our teens. I recently attended our 1943 High School Reunion. They still played "Our Music", and we spoke of "Our War" and all the things that were important to "Our Generation". Unfortunately, the events of "Our Era" may so deeply impact us and effect how we think and feel about issues that we often cannot effectively communicate with people from another generation i.e. "era". The result is that we may live in what I think of as "generational ghettos," passing by those in other generations, each certain that our way is the norm. I do not believe this was God's intent. Instead of being adversaries with other generations (eras), I think we are to help and support one another as we all travel through this journey we call "Life".

In order to start bridging this gap and bringing us together, I believe we first need to understand the basic elements of each generation (era). For illustrative purposes I have prepared the following hypothetical example:

1850–1875	Great-grandparent	Slavery/Civil war
1875-1900	Grandparent	Railroads/Western Expansion
1900–1925	Father	Industrial Expansion/WW I
1925–1950	Me	Depression/WW II
1950–1975	Child	Communism/Civil Rights
1975–2000	Grandchild	Computers/Globalization
2000-2025	Great-grandchild	? ? ?

These may or may not be the definitions that you would use, but they do illustrate some of the great distinctions that must be overcome if we are to live together in harmony. I encourage you to determine your definitions and the characteristics of your era and that of the eras above you and below you in history, so we can all begin to complete—not compete—with one another as we go through life.

The Importance of Good Associations
Our associations also have a great impact on our choices. With the advent of teenage freedom, my circle moved out from my family and school to a broader area of influences. Some were good (such as Boy Scouts and YMCA camp) and some were bad (such as open clubs where alcohol and gambling were available, although unlawful, without much concern for the age of the patrons). I still had some church relationships and occasional Sunday school attendance, but without any real Christian fellowship I continued to struggle between God's call and the pull of a world at war. Right and wrong associations during these impressionable years will have deep

and lasting effects on us for the rest of our lives—and sometimes for eternity.

Beginning to Know Ourselves

When we, as young people, begin to make our teenage choices, it usually causes us to look deeply at ourselves. We become aware of both strengths and weaknesses we see in our lives. I discovered, for example, that I did not like, nor excel, in physical activities and manual work, but I enjoyed and seemed fitted for analytical thinking and word work. I also found that I was conservative even in my teens—choosing a sedate four-door sedan for my first car, while my two brothers drove flashy convertibles. For me, saving money was easy; spending it was hard. I later came to realize that the person who loves money is probably not the one who spends it, but the one who increasingly enjoys saving it and watching it grow! Solomon warns us that amassing silver, gold, and land really ends up being "meaningless, a chasing after the wind." (See Ecclesiastes 2:4–11.) By contrast, storing our treasure in Heaven can bring eternal rewards, as explained in Matthew 6:19–24. I know now, as do many of you, these early choices form patterns we will probably carry all through life and pass on to future generations unless changes are made.

God and the Bible: A Standard for Right and Wrong

Many years ago I attended a small group seminar conducted by Dr. Howard Hendricks in which he spoke of our tendency to live our lives first by the standards of our *Parents*, then by turning to our *Peers*, but that we don't become mature until we begin to base our lives on *Principles*. And, ultimately, these Principles must be based on a *Person*, (i.e., Jesus). I believe the best guide ever given to mankind is Jesus, as revealed to us through His Spirit and His Word—the Bible.

For the Bible, in essence, is a book about choices. Adam and Eve made a poor choice and all succeeding generations have suffered as a result. (See Genesis 3.) Their first two children also faced a choice: Abel chose wisely; Cain chose foolishly, and the consequences of sin haunted him for life. (See Genesis 4.) Moses, in his final address to the Israelites, posed the choice we all face as he urged:

> *This day I call heaven and earth as witnesses against you*
> *that I have set before you life and death, blessings and curses.*
> *Now choose life, so that you and your children may live...*
> (Deuteronomy. 30:19)

Jesus, in a similar vein, closed His great Sermon on the Mount, in Matthew 5-7, with a series of three choices we all face: a narrow or wide gate to enter and a hard or easy road to travel; teachers and trees that do or do not bear fruit; and lives built on a rock so they withstand the storms of life or upon sand so they fall and are destroyed.

At this point let's take a break and let you consider these issues as they relate to your life and the lives of those who are following you.

QUESTIONS

1. What choices did you face during your teens?

2. What were some of the decisions you made, and what influenced you as you made those choices?

3. How would you characterize the era in which you lived during your teen years?

4. How can you help those who follow you understand their era and make good choices during their "Traumatic Teens"?

ADVENTURE
AGE 18–21

The two of them, sent on their way by the Holy Spirit,
went down to Seleucia, and sailed from there to Cyprus.
When they arrived in Salamis,
they proclaimed the word of God in the Jewish synagogues.
John was with them as their helper.
(Acts 13:4–5, emphasis added)

I was 18 years old plus one month and I was on a troop train headed for Air Corps Basic Training at Biloxi, Mississippi. It was September 1943. I didn't know it then, but the next three years would be one of the fastest maturing periods in my life. In order that you can have a more personal sense of what these "Adventure" years meant to me, I have included excerpts of an old WWII Diary at the close of the book. I trust it will give you some idea of the impact this relatively short period of time had on the rest of my life.

I have discovered that time is not constant—neither in the Bible nor in my life. For example, the Israelites were in Egypt about 400 years, and it is a period of silence without significant events being recorded for these people. Then history seemed to explode with Moses and miracles. Within 40 years we had the Exodus, the 10 Commandments and the first five books of the Bible! 1,500 years later Jesus burst on the scene and transformed all of time in three short years!

I believe our lives are like that. Certain periods, such as our adventure years, seem to take on significance far beyond the number of days or years involved. Perhaps our lives are like a description I once heard of learning to fly: "Hours and hours of utter boredom punctuated by moments of stark terror!"

As we approach the end of our teen years, many of us seem to feel the urge to move out and to have an adventure. In some eras we have to plan and make arrangements for this to happen. For our generation it occurred naturally due to the ongoing war. We could either volunteer or most of us would be drafted. I picked the Army Air Corps because I badly wanted to fly and I loved the glamour and excitement it portrayed.

As an example, and to help you think through the adventure years for you, your children, and your grandchildren, let me take you briefly through some of my experiences. I'll try to show certain lessons I learned along the way that may help explain why I think this short period of life can be so important in preparing us for the opportunities and challenges of adulthood.

Leaving Home

When we leave home for an adventure of our own, we cut the cord holding us to childhood. It can often help a young man as he consciously (or unconsciously) struggles to become strong enough to head a new family unit and accept the responsibility to protect and provide for a wife and children of his own. I'm not sure how this leaving home process applies to women. Only men were described in the Bible as leaving their father and mother in Genesis 2:24 and Ephesians 5:31, so I have addressed this from my own male perspective and experience.

For me, leaving home created a healthy loneliness. I still recall the desolation I felt on my first Christmas away from home, standing alone on a street corner in the Michigan town where I was temporarily assigned. But I believe this very loneliness ultimately helps most of us join together with a wife and begin a family of our own. As God said of the first man, Adam, "It is not good for man to be alone" (Gen. 2:18a).

Submission and Discipline

The Air Corps was not a democracy. Our enlistments were for the duration of the war, so we learned patience. We were taught early on to respond to those above us in rank with a pattern of "Yes, Sir!" "No, Sir!" and "No excuse, Sir!"

We slept in unison, marched in unison, ate in unison, showered in unison, wore uniform clothing, and learned to follow orders. Neatness and personal hygiene were not merely suggested but demanded. Obedience and commitment were mandatory, knowing that one day our lives might depend on each of us doing what we had been trained to do and when we were told to do it. Physical and technical training became a part of our lifestyle. And all this permanently marked my life.

Pride and Glory

Recognition is a powerful motivator. Schools use grades and scholarships; athletic teams and companies use awards. And some other institutions use degrees, robes, and titles. The military has long understood and successfully used bars, ribbons, wings, medals, and stripes both to identify and to motivate its participants. I didn't realize at first how deeply this desire for recognition was imbedded in me. I suppose other words to describe the hunger for recognition are "fame" or "glory." But whatever the word, the objective is to get others to look at us and to do so with approval and respect.

This emphasis on personal recognition is the way of the world, but it isn't God's way. It was many years later before I understood that *God* is the one who is to receive the glory. *He* is the one whom we are to acknowledge and praise, rather than seeking recognition for ourselves. The whole universe points to God. As the psalmist says:

> *The heavens declare the glory of God;*
> *the skies proclaim the work of his hands.*
> (Psalm. 19:1)

John the Baptist put it this way: "He [Jesus] must become greater; I must become less" (John 3:30).

I realize now, however, that the war and my adventure were a time that I sought personal recognition and glory. The day I graduated from cadet training and received my navigator wings and second lieutenant bars was one of the sweetest and most memorable of my young life. But my combat career was short, just three missions against oil refinery targets in Japan. The day the war ended, we were out over the Pacific returning from what was apparently the longest flight effort against Japan, as well as the last B-29 air raid of World War II. I was 20 years and four days old.

Sadly, it would be many years before I would understand that God calls us to humility and away from pride. I believe that pride, with its desire for personal recognition and glory, is one of the great sins we pass from generation to generation, despite the fact it is repeatedly condemned throughout the Bible. (See for example Proverbs 8:13, 11:2, 13:10, 16:18, and 29:23.) Placing God and others before ourselves is so difficult, but so necessary if we are to become mature and pass on good rather than evil to those who follow us.

Hopefully, every adventure we pursue, or encourage others to pursue, will be one that ultimately gives the glory to God.

Life and Death
The war made death a common topic. While I was in Bombardier Training in California, I received a call from my father telling me my oldest brother, a Navigator on a B-24 bomber, had been killed in a plane crash over England. In addition our own combat group suffered the loss of six or seven of its 45 aircraft and crews during its training and overseas action. But death for us on a B-29 in the last stages of the war was usually from a distance. We never saw, heard, nor knew those we bombed on the ground. The planes we lost in flights over the ocean were simply gone and never seen again. But trips we made later to bombed-out Manila, or scorched islands such as Iwo Jima, gave us an eerie sense of the total destruction our forces had been waging against our unseen enemy.

Fear and Courage
As we trained on the ground, and later even in the air, there didn't seem to be much feeling of or discussion about fear. Gradually, however, we began to see the constant danger around us. Unsuccessful search missions for crews from airplanes lost

at sea brought home how large the ocean was and how little chance of survival we would have if we were forced to ditch our plane in the water. The long overseas flights from the United States to Guam, and later to Japan, increased my sense of possible problems. But it was bomb runs over enemy targets that really got my attention. Holding steady for several miles on a target up ahead, knowing we couldn't go up, down, or sideways until we reached our "Bombs Away!" point, allowed fears to mount.

It was through these experiences that I learned a valuable lesson: Courage is not the absence of fear, instead it is walking (or flying) on through the fear. One of the most common phrases in the Bible is, "*Fear not!*" I finally realized this phrase was so common because fear is so common to us all. Revelation 21:8 says the "cowardly," and certain others, will go into "the fiery lake." I'm glad it didn't say those who fear. If it did, I don't think there would be many folks in Heaven.

Fear has a way of sending us looking for God and His protection. However, when the threat of imminent disaster subsides, we are often a bit like the heroine I recall in an old World War II movie. She had prayed fervently for her loved one to come home. Then when she looked out the window and saw him getting out of a taxi at her front door, she cried out, "OK, Lord! I can take it from here!"

It would be many years before I would understand that God can take away our anxiety if we rely on Him, pray about everything in advance and thank Him for what He is going to do, as explained in Philippians 4:6–7. Fortunately, the adventure years can move us—and those who love us—to be in prayer on a much more regular basis as we take these first steps into adulthood.

Risk, Responsibility, and Maturity
The basic lesson I see when I look back on this adventure time is that it usually takes risk and responsibility to produce maturity. I believe we rob the next generation of maturity if we refuse to let them take reasonable risks and accept responsibility for their actions.

It's terribly wrenching to let loose of our children after we've spent 15 to 20 years providing for them and protecting them from danger. I recall how my wife and I reacted when one of our sons told us he was going to parachute jump—and then attempt to calm our fears by saying, "But I won't tell you when I'm going to do it so you won't worry." Several weeks later he said, "Well, I did it!"

"What?" I inquired.

"I jumped," he said. And then he added, "And it's really true… Your whole life *does* pass in front of your face!"

This whole experience gave me a little understanding of the fortitude and grace my parents had displayed with three sons in the Air Corps, later known as the Air Force, during wartime. I see now that allowing our children to step out in an adventure helps to mature not only them, but us as well.

The key to all this, I think, is to help the next generation have a *healthy* adventure that may allow reasonable risk but will not produce ugly scars. Unfortunately, a physical war seems to injure us all. It is a time we are dedicated to killing others. Once we begin to violate the principle of life, other principles often are sacrificed as well.

Perhaps a closely supervised mission trip for the purpose of engaging in "*spiritual* warfare" to *save* others may be one good answer. This experience was apparently one of the steps God used to bring young John Mark to maturity as he traveled abroad with Paul and Barnabas, two older, more mature brothers. (See Acts 13:4–5.) This was also true for one young man who was attending a seminar where we were discussing this material. As he listened to this portion of the presentation, he spoke up excitedly and said, in essence, "I urge you all to let your sons have an adventure, even if it means time off from school. Things weren't going so well for me in college, and I went on a short-term mission trip to Mexico. That gave me the desire to go for a year. It changed my life. When I came home, college went well for me. It does mature!"

I arrived home from World War II on July 4, 1946. I called it my Independence Day. When I enrolled at our state university, I found I was entering an era that educators later referred to as the "golden age of education". The reason this educational period was so effective was that the millions of men and women returning to college after years of wartime service were mature far beyond the years of those who normally come directly from high school. I am convinced that an adventure, particularly a healthy one, can be instrumental in helping young men move in a timely way into the next generation.

Let me give you one note of caution: It seems that failure to have a *timely* adventure around the late teens or early twenties may contribute to an *untimely* adventure later in life. I suspect that some sports cars, mid-life flings, and divorces may have part of their roots in the feeling, "Time is running out. I never had my youthful 'adventure,' and I'm going to have it now before it's too late." Unfortunately, the result may be much pain and heartache.

Once again we come to an opportunity for some personal reflection about this time of life for you and for those who are following you.

QUESTIONS

1. Did you have an "Adventure" during this time in your life? If so, describe it and relate its impact on your life.

2. If not describe how you moved (or want to move) into adulthood.

3. How can you help those who follow you have a timely and reasonable "Adventure" to help prepare them for adulthood?

LIFETIME DECISIONS
AGE 21–25

Faith

Therefore everyone who hears these words of mine and puts them into practice is like a wise man who built his house on the rock. The rain came down, the streams rose, and the winds blew and beat against that house; yet it did not fall, because it had its foundation on the rock.
(Matthew 7:24-25)

Marriage

A wife of noble character who can find? She is worth far more than rubies.
(Proverbs 31:10)

Vocation

Then I heard the voice of the Lord saying, "Whom shall I send? And who will go for us?" And I said, "Here am I. Send me!"
(Isaiah 6:8)

As I look back across my life, I see three principal lifetime decisions and three important decision times. I'm sure these decisions and decision times vary for individuals, but for me and for the men I have observed, our lives seemed to often follow this format.

The three decisions concern our *Faith*, our *Marriage*, and our *Vocation*. Some have referred to these as our "Master", our "Mate" and our "Mission". The three decision times often occur toward the end of each generation as we prepare to enter the next season of our lives.

Again, as an example to help you think through your own reaction to these issues and also to be ready to give advice and counsel to those who follow you, let me walk through these three key decisions as I recall them during age 21-25.

Faith—A Foundation for Life

The first and most important issue we face in life is, "What do we believe about God and the reason for our own existence?" At age 21, I was still fighting with God. Self-reliance and the deeply engrained desire to be my own boss, together with the lack of any strong Christian fellowship, kept me on the fringe of the Christian life. I was split between the pull of the world and the call of God. I have since discovered that many of us who do not make a full-blown commitment to Christ by our teenage years often get caught up in the excitement of the world around us that anesthetizes us, at least for a while.

I continued to do some reading and thinking about life, but I did not have a clear understanding of what I believed. The apostle John said that he wrote his gospel,

> ... that you may believe that Jesus is the Christ, the Son of God,
> and that by believing you may have life in his name.
> (John 20:31)

Unfortunately, I either couldn't, or wouldn't, hear that message during this period. My church attendance was sporadic and shallow. The rush of these college years seemed to be a substitute for real faith. Later I would wander through much extraneous literature before God finally revealed Himself and called me to Him through some devout Christian writers.

In the meantime I was without any firm foundation for my life, and it was going to take its toll. We have a little saying in our home, "Start hard, end easy! Start easy, end hard!" How I wish I had made a solid decision for Christ early in my life.

Marriage—A Life Mate

My first date at the university was the young lady who was to be my wife. Bells rang when I saw her, and we became engaged and then married. I was 23 years old. Now, over 60 years later, I realize the marvelous grace of God in allowing me to live most of my life with this partner, friend, and helpmate who has given me more love, joy, and solid counsel than any other person in my life.

Like most young people, my only understanding of marriage was the on-the-job training I received as I watched my parents and other older couples live out their married lives. But I had no real understanding of the proper roles of either a husband or wife. I could not have verbalized what I should be, nor what my wife should be, in order to make our marriage prosper.

It was many years later that I began to study this subject in earnest as God revealed more of my own failures and inadequacies. Also, as I saw our own children moving toward adulthood, I realized I needed to study, try to apply, and then state clearly and unequivocally what I believed the Bible said about the roles of husbands and wives. Only then could I really be of help with this issue.

Much has been written and discussed about our country's current marriage crisis with approximately 50 percent of our marriages failing and about 40 percent of our children being born outside of marriage. I talked with a Christian marriage counselor recently about this growing problem. I asked her if most couples she counseled understood their roles. "Not at all," she responded. "In fact," she said, "We spend a great deal of time and effort trying to get them to put together a list of what each person will do in order to try and make the marriage work."

"How sad," I thought. "We don't provide sufficient training and modeling but, rather, expect each couple, after they are in trouble, to reinvent their own roles of husband and wife." With the marked decrease in healthy husband and wife models, and the lack of any solid marriage training for much of our society, it is becoming increasingly difficult for many young people to know what they should be and do in a marriage relationship, and also what to look for in a prospective spouse.

Some time ago I was a facilitator for several college students at a leadership conference. After two days together, I noticed that none of the young men and women had spoken at all about marriage and family. Instead, they devoted all their discussion to their outside careers. Finally, I asked, "Which do you believe is harder, an outside career or marriage?" They unanimously said, "Marriage!" It turned out over half of them had a parent who had been through divorce, and they felt very uncomfortable discussing or even contemplating marriage for themselves.

I asked another group of young twenty-something Christians if they believed their generation would like to know the biblical roles of husband and wife. "Yes," they responded. Then one added, "We do want it if it's from the Bible, but we don't want to know what our parents' generation thinks are proper roles, because we don't believe they have done a good job." What an indictment!

More and more young people seem to be delaying marriage, feeling unsure of their roles and concerned that, statistically, they do not have a good chance of staying together for life. Isn't it incumbent upon each parent and grandparent in the Christian community to study and then try to live and to teach the Biblical roles of husband and wife if we are to recover the Biblical institution of marriage for the generations who follow us?

Vocation—A Life Work

Our vocation is our "calling," that I sometimes refer to as our "voca" (as in "vocal"). Unfortunately, there may be a great difference between our calling from God and the job we perform in the workplace. Someone has divided our vocations into empire-building for this world and Kingdom building for eternity. Most of our years of schooling are directed toward making us proficient in our worldly trade, business, or profession, and virtually none is directed toward hearing and responding to the call of God.

How I would have profited from hearing early in life the words of Ephesians 2:10,

> *For we are God's workmanship, created in Christ Jesus*
> *to do good works, which God prepared in advance for us to do.*

How much it would mean for us to know during our college years that God has made us perfect for the work He created for us to do, and that our role is to listen for His call and then to respond, *"Here am I. Send me!"*

I entered the field of law because I was a word person and others I respected encouraged me in that direction. I enjoyed the study of law. I readily understood it was a good and honorable profession that could be applied to do good in this world; but I did not see nor understand until many years later how it might be used to build God's Kingdom.

There is a thrill in studying intensely and finally receiving an advanced degree. But I have found it is nothing compared to the thrill and fulfillment of being called and prepared by God to use this knowledge and degree and everything else God has given us to help in the building of His Kingdom rather than worldly empires!

I think Peter understood this concept when he first met Jesus, shortly after Peter had finished an unsuccessful night of fishing. Jesus first demonstrated His control of worldly success by telling Peter where to throw his nets for a record catch—so large the nets began to break and the boats began to sink. Then Jesus immediately invited Peter and his brother Andrew to leave it all:

"Come, follow me," Jesus said,
"and I will make you fishers of men."
(Matthew 4:19)

A short time ago, one of my sons startled me with the question, "Your work wasn't all that important to you, was it?" After practicing law (which I thoroughly enjoyed) for over 40 years, I at first started to insist that he was wrong. But as I slowly reflected, I finally responded, "You're right. It was the people and God's word that have been important." My work was, of course, very important, *at that time*, as a building block God was using in my life. But it was *not the major purpose in life* that I felt it to be earlier in my life.

I am convinced that we need to work to survive in this world, as stated in 2 Thessalonians 3:10, but I have also discovered that we need to keep this world and eternity in proper perspective.

As Paul instructs his young protégé, Timothy:

For physical training is of some value,
but godliness has value for all things,
holding promise for both the present life
and the life to come.
(I Timothy 4:8)

In other words this world is important, but it is only part of eternity. Therefore, I have concluded we need to prepare and then major in Kingdom building and not just our secular work. When we do that, Jesus assures us He will see that all our physical needs are met:

But seek first his kingdom and his righteousness,
and all these things [i.e., worldly needs] *will be given to you as well.*
(Matthew 6:33)

Now it's time to give you an opportunity to reflect on the following questions as they pertain to your journey and the journeys of those ahead of you and behind you in life during these closing years of Generation I. It may help if you first review the Life Line at the back of the book and trace your life journey up through Age 25.

QUESTIONS

What Lifetime Decisions have you made, (or do you want to make,) in each of the following areas:

1. Faith

2. Marriage

3. Vocation

Generation II:
A Time To Do
Age 25–50

When I was a child, I talked like a child,
I thought like a child, I reasoned like a child.
When I became a man, I put childish ways behind me.
(1 Corinthians 13:11)

These are the productive years—the summer of our life. This is the time when we move from being a child, to being a parent. These are the years during which we usually put into action all that we have learned and have been building during the preceding generation. These are often the busy years as we engage in the frenzy of activities so common to this period of life.

INTO THE WORLD
AGE 25–30

As you sent me into the world,
I have sent them into the world.
(John 17:18)

As we begin Generation II, we often find ourselves thrust out into the world. If we have lived a rather sheltered life in Generation I, this may be a difficult time. But it is also often a time of exciting change. I would have found it helpful if I had known that there were actually *four* worlds that I needed to understand and fit in with during life. In order to aid you as you work through this transition, let me describe each of the institutions that I believe God has ordained to govern these four worlds and make some comments that I hope may help you in your journey.

The Four Institutions
I believe the four institutions are: *Family; Church; Workplace; and Government.* (See Ephesians 4–6, Colossians 3, Romans 13, 1 Timothy 2–6, and 1 Peter 2–5.) Each of these four institutions has a special purpose and emphasis to help us individually, and as a society, to function best and to live orderly lives in this world God has entrusted to us.

1. Family—Propagation: To carry on life
Only the Family is ordained by God, in scripture, to produce people—the Church doesn't, the Workplace doesn't, and the Government doesn't. Instead, each of these other three institutions need and use the people produced by Families to carry on their work. In recent years our emphasis on careers

outside the Family, for both men and women, has diminished the perceived value of full time service to our Family. We give lip service to family life, but many parents—Christian and non-Christian—encourage both young men and young women to concentrate their lives in one of the other three institutions. As a result, our birthrate has dropped.

Despite the repeated Biblical command to multiply (e.g. Genesis 1:28; Jeremiah 29:6), we have relied in recent years on increasing longevity and high immigration to sustain our population. Although there is a popular cry to further limit family growth, the sad fact is that—while some areas of the nonindustrial world are rapidly gaining population—we in the United States seem to be barely reproducing ourselves. And birth rates are negative in parts of the world (e.g. Japan and Italy)!

We need the family.

2. Church—Purpose: To deal with the meaning of life

Down through the ages, the Church has centered its mission on determining and acting upon the reason and purpose for life. While there is much overlapping among the four institutions, only the Church has uniquely dealt with such questions as, "Why was I born? Who is God? Is there eternal life, and judgment, after this life is over?" It is the institution of the Church that codified the writings that answer these questions in the book we call the Bible. And only the institution of the Church continues to wrestle with these eternal spiritual issues in every generation.

We need the Church.

3. Workplace—Production: To sustain and improve life
Although profit is necessary to survive, the primary purpose of
the Workplace is production. We need profit, but that is to be
a result and not the purpose of our work. Only the Workplace
produces the physical goods and services we need to live—
the Family doesn't (although it provides the people who
do the production in the Workplace); the Church doesn't; and
the Government doesn't. Instead, these other three institutions
live off the goods and services produced in the workplace, just
as the institutions of church, workplace, and government utilize
the people produced by the family.

We need the Workplace.

4. Government—Protection: To protect life
Although the Government, in recent years has become a provider
for much of our population (by taxing some to distribute to
many), its Biblical role is to be a protector (e.g. I Timothy 2:1-2;
I Peter 2:13-14). Only the Government has the overarching
authority and power to keep peace among its constituent
citizens and domestic institutions. And only the Government
has the resources and capability to defend us all from outside
aggression. The Family doesn't; the Church doesn't; and the
Workplace doesn't.

We need the Government.

Balance
Although we need all four institutions, we also need them
to be in balance. In recent years we have seen an obvious

over-emphasis in our society on the Workplace and the Government with a decreasing emphasis on the Family and the Church. I recently spoke about these issues to a group of about 150 college students. They were largely Christian, young men and women called together in a conference to discuss *"Faith and Values"*. I asked them to take an informal poll so we could see the institutions in which they intended to carry out their life work. About one half said, the Workplace; about 25 percent said, the Government, and about 15 percent said, the Church. I asked lastly about the Family, and only about five or six hands went up!

The institution of the Family under-girds the other three institutions and is the foundation of all society. Today, we are cannibalizing the Family and using the people it produces to operate the Workplace, the Government, and the Church, while the Family itself is stumbling with divorce, illegitimacy, and turmoil. Unless a sufficient number of believers understand the value of the Family and are willing to make this institution their major life work, rather than prioritizing careers in the Workplace, the Government or the Church, the Family crisis may worsen and ultimately destroy all four institutions.

We need Balance among all four of these institutions.

Christ in Us and Us in the World

I believe the four institutions of Family, Church, Workplace and Government are also the four great mission fields of life. Each of us has a role to play in one or more of these areas as we work out the special emphasis and purpose of our individual lives. (See Colossians 1:25–29.)

Deep inside each of us is a core passion, the driving force of our lives. There is something we hold more important than anything else. And what is at our core will flow out of us into every institution where we live out our lives. Whether our primary passion is fame, money, sex, power, business, politics, family, golf, or God, that passion will ultimately affect all that we are and everything and everyone we touch. As one older man I met at a conference put it, "What we feed the most, grows the most!"

As I approach the end of my journey, I realize that my deepest desire is to keep God (Father, Son and Holy Spirit) at the core of my life. Often I fail to keep centered on that fact, but that is my desire. I am now confident that when we get out of God's way, our lives can and should look like the following diagram as He moves through us out into the world He came to serve and to save:

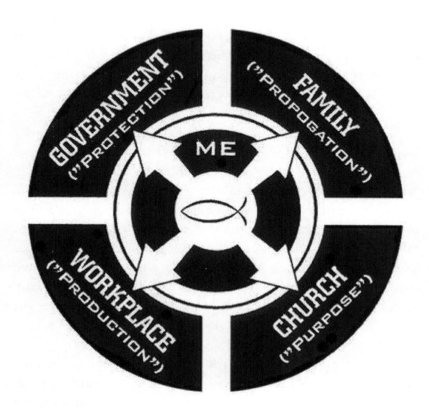

God wants us all to place Him at the core of our lives and then be used where and how He directs. I suspect it has been—or will be—a long, arduous, bumpy process for most of you who are reading this book. It has been for me. For that reason, let me make a few observations that may be helpful about each of these areas.

1. Family

Most of my understanding of Family life came from tradition and not from scripture. Fortunately, I had some good, although not perfect, early role models. Unfortunately, I still made many mistakes. I believe these mistakes might have been largely avoided if I had worked through the Biblical roles of husbands and wives in advance—or even as we moved through those early years—rather than delaying until most of our children were nearly grown. I urge you not to wait!

In addition, my father died when I was 26 years old so I no longer had any elder figure in my family. I realize now that I, unconsciously, reached out to my father-in-law (and after his death to a few other older men whom we will discuss later) to fill this void. I encourage any of you who are left alone in an area of life to find surrogate physical, spiritual, business, and professional advisors when they are absent from your life.

2. Church

I had no strong Christian fellowship or model during these early years. Because we were floundering and I had no doctrinal background to guide us, we simply looked for a Church we enjoyed. At first we were drawn to one where our infant daughter seemed satisfied and didn't cry in the nursery. Later, we were attracted to a new fledgling church that was being started by a dedicated pastor who reached out to us and prayed openly with us when he first visited our home. This was a dramatic and entirely foreign experience that affected us deeply. We joined shortly thereafter. The pastors and people in this church blessed our lives immeasurably over the years. They were part of the process God used to bring us closer to Him. I encourage you to find a church that relies on Jesus, His Father, His Spirit and His Word. Then make it a meaningful part of your life. Don't delay. Otherwise you may do as I did and simply float for many years in your spiritual journey, without direction or growth.

3. Workplace

After graduating from Law School in 1951, I quickly found I was *not* a fully trained lawyer. I had been given a foundation of theory and knowledge, but I needed at least three to five years of practical experience and on-the-job training before I could function on my own as an attorney.

I believe we all need a time of apprenticeship as we begin a new area of work. And it seems to be an immutable law that, just as our early training by our parents sets the values and disciplines that affect our thoughts and actions throughout all our lives, so our initial bosses have great influence on the values and disciplines we will use throughout our work lives. While we cannot choose our parents, it is important that we try and choose carefully those who will train and disciple us during the early years of our careers.

My first job after Law School was with a sole practitioner in his 40's. Our office was in a large downtown office building, which in those days had spittoons in the hallways and elevator operators running the elevators. One of my first assignments was to probate the estate of the doctor who brought me into the world! Life is a continuum.

My boss was a business-oriented lawyer who trained me well in business and probate law. But he made it clear from the beginning that he had hired me to handle any litigation we had, so I was on my own as a trial lawyer. I know I missed a great deal not having a trainer to instruct me in trial work, but it also taught me a valuable lesson: if we don't have a trainer, go find one! For me it meant going to the courthouse and watching trials being conducted by experienced trial lawyers, and joining forces with other firms when necessary. I have concluded that many of us may not have formal trainers to apprentice us in certain areas, (including parents and grandparents, as I mentioned before), but there are usually substitutes around if we will look for them and ask for guidance.

My employer was an honest man. I have always been grateful he modeled ethical behavior and never asked me to do anything improper or questionable. In those days our code of ethics was summarized on one sheet of paper. I think it was best characterized by a story I heard about an older, respected attorney in our city who was asked to attend a firm meeting to decide if some proposed action was ethical. He entered the room and announced, in essence, "If we have to meet to talk about whether it is ethical, then we won't do it!" That's ethics!

Although there have been many advancements in the intervening years (e.g., more racial justice), it has been heartbreaking to see the gradual erosion of many moral and ethical standards and principles. As one perceptive man noted, "The unthinkable becomes thinkable; the thinkable becomes doable; and the doable becomes the norm!" And worst of all is to realize some younger people believe they are doing right because that's the way they were trained in the early years of their business or professional lives. Be careful, therefore, who trains you as you begin your career in the Workplace. And encourage those who follow you to do the same.

4. Government

Because I practiced law I was deeply involved in the judicial branch of Government, but I was not involved in making the laws or in executing them. Because these also have tremendous impact on our private and public lives, I sometimes feel I should have been more involved in these other two areas, also. But we can't do it all. I do encourage you to be involved in some way, because the institution of Government is too important to be neglected or ignored.

Once again we come to a time for personal application. I hope these comments have sparked your memory—or your hopes if you have not yet lived through these years—and that you will spend some time considering the issues we have been discussing.

QUESTIONS

1. Who or what is the "God" at the central core of your life? In other words, what is your driving force?

2. How do you want to be involved in the "Family?"

3. How do you want to be involved in the "Church?"

4. How do you want to be involved in the "Workplace?"

5. How do you want to be involved the in "Government?"

ON OUR OWN
AGE 30–35

*Joseph was thirty years old
when he entered the service of Pharaoh king of Egypt.*
(Genesis 41:46)

*David was thirty years old
when he became king, and he reigned forty years.*
(II Samuel 5:4)

*Now Jesus himself was about thirty years old
when he began his ministry.*
(Luke 3:23a)

For thousands of years, age thirty was an important threshold in the scriptures. It marked the beginning of the mature ministries of Joseph (around 2000 BC), David (about 1000 BC), and Jesus, a thousand years later. It was also the age set for beginning the work assignments for various Levite clans, about 1500 BC:

*Count all the men from thirty to fifty years of age
who come to serve in the work in the Tent of Meeting.*
(Numbers 4:3, see also verses 23, 30, 35, 39, and 43)

Personal Reflections
Looking back I see that this timetable was also applicable for my own life and the lives of many others around me. At age thirty I opened a law office, and I was joined almost immediately by another young attorney. I had a wife, three small children, about $300, a few small clients, and lots of hope.

It is much easier and more comfortable to reminisce about those early years than it was to live them. As has been said, "War stories are more fun than wars!" But to encourage you in your own recollections, let me share a favorite story of an early client.

One of my first major clients was a family business of a young friend. He was taking responsibility for their company and wanted to build his own team. I will never forget the day he brought his father to discuss our representation of their company. What must that older gentleman have thought as he entered my small office, with its used desk and two wooden straight-back chairs? Here he was, talking with a young, relatively inexperienced, lawyer about to be entrusted with the legal responsibility for the company he had been building for many years. As I had expected, my friend indicated he wanted to use our firm as he went forward with managing the company. His father's reply was classic. "That's all right, Son," he said. "But what will we do if we have a *problem?*"

It was many years before I realized I had learned two very valuable lessons. First was the encouragement I received from my young friend's willingness to trust me before I was established. But an even more important lesson was the example of his father's courage in taking a risk so that the next generation could move forward. Fortunately for all of us, this shaky start produced a successful association of over forty years.

The five years from age 30 to 35 became a very important chapter in my life. Being able to do the work we want to do, with people we like, and in a location we enjoy, is truly one of life's pearls. Work is not an evil to be endured. Instead it is a great part of why we were born. It was given to man for his good before the fall of Adam. (See Genesis 2:15.) While sin has made the conditions surrounding work more difficult, work itself is one of God's choicest gifts. As Solomon concluded,

> *A man can do nothing better than to eat and drink*
> *and find satisfaction in his work.*
> *This too, I see, is from the hand of God...*
> (Ecclesiastes 2:24)

Being on our own doesn't mean we literally have to open our own personal workplace. It simply means we have been trained and experienced to the point that we can now serve by ourselves in our chosen field of work. We can be turned loose on society without being a danger to ourselves or to others!

It was during these years I began to experience the great excitement and fulfillment of practicing law on my own. I'll never forget my first jury trial. I suddenly realized the judge at his bench, the jury in their box, the witness in the stand, and me speaking in the courtroom were all real. I almost panicked, for a moment, as the comprehension of the event hit home.

It's much like flying an airplane. For those of you who have soloed, you know the almost drug-like sensation the first time you take off the ground—totally alone—and know you are on your own. Your foot may shake, but after long training and dual instruction you are airborne—alone!

Good News and Bad News

These years are a combination of good news and bad news. The good news is we have self-confidence, so we begin to step out into new areas. We are the Young Turks who see the old ways passing and know it is time for changes, and we want to help them happen. Like Elihu, the young man who spoke with Job, the need to speak out finally builds until we feel we will burst if we don't do so. (See Job 32:1–20.) We innovate. We build on the past, but we also move out into unknown areas without knowing enough to be afraid.

It is a time of action that requires great fire and energy. I recently listened to a 60-yearold business veteran describing his second start-up company. He warned, "If you don't have the fire in the belly you had at age 30, don't try it!" It's true. It is usually the risk and innovation we take during our thirties that we hone in our forties and mature and pass on to others during our fifties and beyond.

Just as we seem to need an adventure around age 20 to mature us for the responsibilities of adult life, so do we often need to be on our own in our work world to help us become mature in the work God has called us to complete. That's the good news.

The bad news is in two parts. The first problem is we often won't listen during these years. While it isn't true for everyone, I have discovered that many people (including myself) from about age 30 to 35 want to do things our own way—even if we fail. Too often we are like the young lawyer who responded to an overly helpful judge, "Please, Judge, I would like to lose this case in my own way!"

68

It's almost as if there were a dozen doors in front of us, and we want to open each door ourselves in order to experience life firsthand, rather than relying on the experiences of those who have gone before us. As a result, we can waste much valuable time. And we can be hurt—sometimes, badly.

There is a Godly wisdom of the ages we all need if we are to be and do all God wants in the time He has allocated to us on this earth. We can't, of course, rely merely on our parents, our peers, or the wise men of this age. But we can rely on God's wisdom of the ages to save ourselves—and others around us and following us—much time, effort, and grief. It is wise to read about Joseph in 2000 BC, David in 1000 BC, and Jesus at the change point in history two thousand years ago, as well as studying the lives and writings of other saints over the years. It helps us become wise to study those who have gone before. It gives us a great sweep of history—not merely a narrow keyhole view from our small limited perspective of the short, plus or minus 100 year span of life we are granted.

The wisdom of God is for all ages and places. It is different from the warped traditions of a family or a culture. As the apostle, Paul, warns,

> *See to it that no one takes you captive through hollow and*
> *deceptive philosophy, which depends on human tradition and the*
> *basic principles of this world rather than on Christ.*
> (Colossians 2:8)

I encourage you, therefore, to read histories and biographies—particularly in the Bible. Maturity doesn't mean we don't make mistakes. It does mean taking faith-stretching risks to meet the needs God shows us—but always based on the wisdom of God in his Word, the guidance of the Holy Spirit in our lives, the counsel of Godly believers and our own intellect, prayers, and experiences.

Now we come to the other part of the bad news. The problem, simply stated, is that we can come to enjoy our work too much. There is a great deal of pride, fulfillment, and fun in doing good work—especially when we are rewarded with money, perks, position, or praise. In addition, those of us who work in the competitive market place realize there is a rush that comes from winning that can become almost addictive.

By contrast, there is a great deal of humility and even pain when we allow God to work through us while being sure that the credit goes to *Him* and not to us! Paul warns us we will either be a slave to righteousness and Christ, or a slave to sin and death (e.g. Romans 6). Thus, even though we are living on our own, we have a lifelong struggle whether to serve God and others or to serve ourselves. Being on our own gives us freedom to choose our course. It is important that we recognize this responsibility early and that we use our work and our lives to listen—and then move closer to God and His plan for our lives.

One Final Observation

Age 30-35 seems to be a window of opportunity; a chance to move out into the fullness of life God has for us. But it doesn't follow that everyone will have this same timetable, either in the scriptures or in modern life. Life isn't over if we aren't on our own by age 35. The Bible and history have numerous examples of people who began their ministries at other times. But the examples of men like Joseph, David and our Lord Jesus, together with other saints and my own experience and observations have convinced me that age 30 to 35 is a unique time. We should watch this time period carefully, both for ourselves and for others who may be following us, so we can all think seriously about stepping out into maturity as we go through this age period.

Here are some questions that may help.

QUESTIONS

1. Where are you going "On your Own"? Are you (or were you) moving closer to the world or closer to God?

2. Write down a short list of those from whom you can learn. Also jot down any books, or topics, that could help you in your journey. Choose a few to pursue.

3. Consider the importance you place in your work. Can it become addictive to you? How can you give the credit to God for all that happens?

4. What do you want to model for those who are following you?

STRIVING FOR SUCCESS
AGE 35–40

Yet when I surveyed all that my hands had done and what I had toiled to achieve, everything was meaningless, a chasing after the wind; nothing was gained under the sun.

(Ecclesiastes 2:11)

These are the running years when we try to do it all. In writing Ecclesiastes, Solomon speaks nine times of *"chasing the wind."* Did you ever think of chasing the wind and trying to catch it? There are two problems: we often can't run fast enough and, even if we could, we can't catch the wind and hold it no matter how hard we strive.

I believe Solomon was simply saying, "I spent my life chasing things I could not catch!" Read Ecclesiastes 2:1–11 and hear the cry of futility voiced by this renowned, wealthy, and wise king because he finally concluded he had been "chasing the wind." A little poem says it well:

I worked night and day,
What my eyes saw I had.
I denied myself nothing,
But still I felt sad.

For whoever loves money,
Never gets quite enough;
And appetites get bigger,
The more they are stuffed!

I've come to realize that chasing the wind is a common malady, whether we lived 3000 years ago when Ecclesiastes was written or today. And as I review my own life and the lives of others, this problem often seems to reach its peak as we approach the midpoint of Generation II.

As I mentioned earlier, I believe about halfway through each generation we often become aware that our present chapter is going to come to an end, and we do not feel prepared for what lies ahead. It can unnerve us and cause us great consternation. These years often produce some of the most turbulent rapids and rough waters we experience as we travel through life.

You will recall that about halfway through Generation I, usually around age 12-13, we hit puberty and many of us tumbled into the chaotic teen years. We usually struggle through, but sometimes we have lasting scars. Now, halfway through Generation II (often around age 37-38) the process can start again. This time, however, instead of dealing with puberty and coming *into* adult life, we can come to the startling awareness that our life will someday be *over*. We are not immortal! We look ahead and, for the first time, we see life is swiftly moving by, and we aren't sure we are where we hoped to be, or even ought to be.

We have studied, trained, gone "on our own", and we want to be sure we have "success" while there is still time. So we begin to run all the harder. During these years our greatest shortage seems to be time itself.

Ironically, we now begin to feel the twinge of age. We don't run so fast, or play basketball quite so easily. Our hair may be a little thinner, or grayer, or we may be a little paunchier. And the term "40-year-old" may take on an ominous and very personal tone. As a result, we often deal with the problem just as Solomon did hundreds of years before Christ, and countless others have done through the ages: we *strive for success*. We now make every effort to live our lives to the fullest and leave our mark on history while there is still time.

Worldly Success
Unfortunately success, in the eyes of the world, is commonly spelled "M-O-R-E." Corporately and individually the goal, too often, is to acquire and enjoy more and to become larger and more important. As a bumper sticker suggested, "Whoever dies with the most toys, wins!"

I spoke with the CEO of a large institution and asked the purpose for their organization. Without hesitation, he replied, "To get bigger!" In our era of merger-mania, bigger seems generally accepted as better.

We as individuals are not immune to this same weakness. We strive for more money, more prestige, more fame, more pleasure, and more property. For a while we feel normal rather than guilty. Everybody's doing it. As one old farmer said in self-defense, "I don't want all the land, just that which adjoins mine!" But, gradually, we begin to feel that something is wrong. We have a growing sense that maybe, just maybe, we, too, are chasing the wind!

Real Success
Some years ago we were attending a dinner party given by some friends. During the evening the hostess's mother, who was a generation older, drew me aside to talk. She asked me two very

provocative questions. One we will discuss later, but the first question fits here. She said to me, "There are two questions you'll have to ask yourself in life, Marvin. The first is, 'What is your definition of success?'"

At some point, each of us has to decide our definition of success. Whatever that may be, it will become our goal and dramatically affect our life. Later, I'm going to ask you for your definition, so I will give you mine now: "That I might be used by God to be and do what He had planned for me". It has absolutely nothing to do with the size of my bank account or my organization(s), nor what degrees I've obtained, offices I've held, or awards I've received. Success, to me, only has to answer the question, "Am I becoming the person, and doing the work, God has planned for me?" If so, I believe I'm successful; if not, I need to change.

I believe we were all created for a purpose. For example, when Jesus was asked if he was king of the Jews, he responded,

> *...for this reason I was born...*
> (John 18:37b)

The prophet Jeremiah had a similar understanding:

> *The word of the LORD came to me, saying, "Before I formed you in the womb I knew you, before you were born I set you apart; I appointed you as a prophet to the nations."*
> (Jeremiah 1:4-5)

Psalm 139:16 reflects this conclusion for each of us:

...your eyes saw my unformed body. All the days ordained for me were written in your book before one of them came to be.

In the New Testament, Ephesians 2:10 says it this way:

For we are God's workmanship, created in Christ Jesus to do good works, which God prepared in advance for us to do.

Real success comes when God's will, not mine, is done and when God is glorified, not me. As John the Baptist said,

He must become greater; I must become less.
(John 3:30)

Here let me mention some traps I believe can keep us from real success.

The *first trap*, of course, is simply to seek worldly success, instead of real success. When we choose this route we, along with others, suffer as a result.

A *second trap* is that our drive for success in one area may contribute to our failure in another area. The divorce courts are grim recorders of many who become so intense, as they try to succeed in their careers, their marriages fail.

Finally, there is one more very subtle trap I want to discuss—doing good, but for the wrong reason. I believe one way that trap is sprung is when we accept altruistic egoism as real success. While this concept is an improvement over many of the world's systems, I do not believe it is God's *best*. Altruistic egoism embraces the thought that I will help you succeed in order that I may succeed in the process. Thus, I do good work for you, but *my underlying goal is to reward myself* with money, reputation, or other personal benefits. The resulting work is good and we both receive some worldly benefits.

However, you and I and the world around us all miss an eternal benefit when we live according to altruistic egoism. We miss the pull toward God that occurs when we do right for the best reason—that God might be glorified! First Corinthians 10:31 reminds us:

> *So whether you eat or drink or whatever you do,*
> *do it all for the glory of God.*

In fact, God's way may *not* necessarily result in my betterment *in this world.* Jesus promises us persecution. (See John 15:18–20.) Peter warns us in 1 Peter 2:20–21 and 3:17 that we may actually suffer for doing good. And Paul tells us that the apostles themselves became "the scum of the earth, the refuse of the world". (I Corinthians 4:13b)

But all this suffering occurs so that God may be glorified. What an impact it has when we do good—even though it does not, and probably will not, accrue to our benefit. Instead we may be reviled, hated, or persecuted! After reciting our need to follow Christ's example of being willing to suffer for doing good, Peter concludes,

Always be prepared to give an answer to everyone who asks you to give the reason for the hope that you have.
(I Peter 3:15b)

In other words, our suffering may glorify God and cause another person to become curious, ask, and become reconciled back to the family of God. Perhaps Peter understood this so well because Jesus had told him to leave his bountiful fish harvest, lay down his net, and follow Jesus, who promised then to make Peter and his companions "fishers of men." (See Matthew 4:19.)

This is *real* success—to be involved in building God's kingdom for God's glory without regard to our personal benefit. We do our work out of gratitude, because He has already saved us, and we want to bless Him with our lives. When we live in this way, we get to share in His work. That's real success!

Now here are some questions that may help you analyze these issues as they relate to your own life journey.

QUESTIONS

1. What is your definition of "Success"?

2. Are you following God or "chasing the wind?"

3. How can you help yourself and the next generations have "real" Success?

SURRENDER
AGE 40–45

The jailer called for lights, rushed in and fell trembling before
Paul and Silas.
He then brought them out and asked, "Sirs, what must I do to be saved?"
They replied, "Believe in the Lord Jesus, and you will be saved—
you and your household."
(Acts 16:29–31)

Crisis Number Two

Some have called this period of a person's life, the "Funky Forties". Others have referred to it as our "Mid-Life-Crisis". A speaker I once heard went even further and entitled his talk, *Middle Age, A **Normal** Crisis*. But whatever we call these years, many people—including myself—have found them to be a challenging, and sometimes chaotic, part of our lives. Perhaps tracing our course up to this point in our journey will help us understand why this often happens.

As we move out of our teens and begin to find our way through the end of Generation I, many of us find our confidence seems to grow; and by the time we reach age 25 our life journey has often returned to normal. The next ten to fifteen years may be quite upbeat as we become fully trained, then able to work on our own, and finally start to taste success. When that happens, our chart often looks like this:

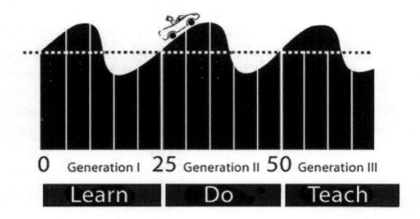

0   Generation I   25 Generation II 50 Generation III

Learn   Do   Teach

Then everything begins to change. Life, once again, often seems to be rocky, almost out of control. As one man who had experienced this difficult time put it, "It doesn't just move downward—*it drops straight down!*" If that happens the roller-coaster points downhill again, and now the chart may begin to look like this:

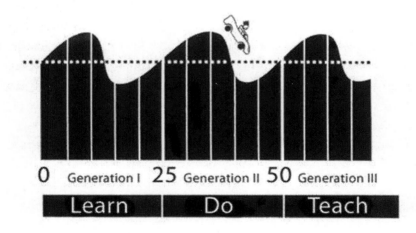

0   Generation I   25 Generation II 50 Generation III

Learn   Do   Teach

Let me mention here what I have come to believe is one of God's great ironies in life. *At the time of our "Funky Forties," our children are often in their "Traumatic Teens" and our parents may be struggling through the "Sobering Sixties"*! After I noticed this strange convergence, I often wondered, "Why?" I still don't know. Perhaps it is because we are more compassionate with the problems of others when we, too, hurt. (See 2 Corinthians 1:3–4.) But, unfortunately, we may each become so absorbed in our own dilemma that we aren't too helpful with the other two generations' difficulties.

Another possibility is that it is all part of the maturing process in our lives. I am convinced God gives children—and particularly teenagers—to parents, partly to help the *parents* grow up. There is something very maturing about going through the teen years ourselves, and then bleeding vicariously as our children suffer through this same period. Much of the time they must find their own way, for we can no longer kiss the hurt and make it well as we could with their childhood bumps and scratches. Perhaps that reality, combined with watching our aged parents struggle through their own late-in-life crisis, as they approach the end of Generation III and the beginning of old age, is necessary for us to complete our growing up process.

Not everyone, of course, has all these experiences or has them occur at neat and precise times. But my experience is that they are a likely enough phenomena that we should consider them as we chart our way through life.

Delayed "Adventures"

I believe we react in many different ways during these periods, based at least partly on what has transpired in our own lives. Let me repeat the warning signal we discussed briefly in the *Adventure* chapter, that is the possibility that some men, consciously or unconsciously, feel they were cheated in their early years, so they may set out around age 40 to have their adventure now. It appears some sports cars are purchased, or other untimely actions are taken, during these years in a belated effort to have it all before it's too late and life passes us by. Unfortunately, incalculable hurt, including broken marriages and families, are sometimes the result.

The Bible says, "There is a time for everything", but also notes that everything is "beautiful in its time" (Ecclesiastes. 3:1, 11). When we try to live as a "teen" when we are age 40, or as a 40 year old when we are a teenager, it usually won't work. Time has a way of refusing to budge. It may bend for awhile, but ultimately time will have its way.

Maturity and Time

Another interesting fact is that our degree of maturity seems directly connected to our view of time. As we noted in Generation I, six months seems a long time when we are quite young. Even by the time we reach age 25, we are often able to comprehend only about 25 years into the future (i.e. to the end of Generation II). But as we gradually move through Generation II, we usually become mature enough to grasp the whole hundred or so years of our lifetime. I suppose that's why we sometimes panic around age 40 when we realize time is running out for us, and that we too will come to the end! But even then, we may not think much important happened before we were born or will happen after we die. That often appears to be left for Generations III and IV we will discuss later.

Revisiting Our Lifetime Decisions

Robert Hicks has written a helpful book, *The Masculine Journey*, in which he identifies six stages of manhood. These include the "warrior," who may become wounded as he engages in the battles men fight during these high-energy years. This corresponds with my own experiences. I, too, found that some men have been wounded—sometimes quite badly—by the time they are in their 40's. These wounds may occur because of a difficult experience, such as losing a job, a promotion, a marriage, or some other dream.

During these years we may begin to feel that life *is* running out. We often sense we are rapidly becoming what we're going to be, and it may not be what we wanted or hoped. We may feel frustrated, bewildered, and sometimes broken. But a positive effect of these times is that they tend to force us to revisit and reevaluate the three lifetime decisions we discussed earlier: our Faith, our Marriage, and our Vocation (i.e. "Master", "Mate" and "Mission"). How we handle these three issues now can greatly affect the rest of our lives and the lives of those around us and of those who follow us. Because of this, let me share with you my own testimony of some profound experiences that altered my life for eternity.

My Testimony

As we approached the last of the 1960s, I sensed that my spiritual journey was about to reach a turning point. The struggle had been growing with increasing intensity over the preceding years. As I had attempted to play out the role of what I should be to satisfy both myself and the people in my life, I had gradually become a compartmentalized, fractured person. Deep down I recognized that the person I was trying to build was not truly adequate, nor complete. I was becoming painfully aware that life was deeper and more meaningful than the small world I had built around myself.

During these years I met no Christian in the workplace whose lifestyle made a significant impact on me. While such persons were undoubtedly present, I was not aware of them. As the Bible says,

For this people's heart has become calloused; they hardly hear with their ears,
and they have closed their eyes. Otherwise they might see with their eyes,
hear with their ears, understand with their hearts and turn,
and I would heal them.
(Matthew. 13:15)

From my closed position, it seemed no one was able concurrently to speak out and live out the principles of the Christian faith in real life. I saw full-time, professional Christians who were expected to be Holy, but for the rest of us, our work worlds seemed to operate on the hard realities of life that might or might not conform to scriptural principles. Gradually, my quest took me into books that had been written by others whose search paralleled my own. I finally realized that I was on the threshold of the eternal question that all of us must ultimately face, "What is the real purpose of life—and death?"

I discovered there were two answers to that question—mine and God's. My answer was to try and use life to satisfy my own present desires through pleasure, position, power, and possessions. The quest for these temporary goals also became the anesthetic that I used to shield myself from facing the question of eternity and how I would spend it. By contrast, God wanted me to desire Him and allow Him to lead me to those things that would provide not only present necessities, but also eternal purpose and meaning to my life and the activities in which I was engaged. But I was afraid to let go of the old in order to grab hold of the new. For years I wrestled with God. Gradually I began to realize, especially through the writings of certain authors, that it was a test of the will. Either God's will or my will was going to rule my life, and it had to be a total, unconditional surrender!

Finally, in true labor lawyer style, I negotiated a settlement with Him. I couldn't bring myself to surrender my will in one step, but I agreed in the early summer of 1969 that I would surrender on August 10, 1969, my 44th birthday. As each day passed, it seemed a part of the countdown to my own execution, which it was. As a friend explained later, "Don't you see; you have to die to yourself before you can be 'born again!'"

My birthday finally arrived. Following a celebration with my family— and without advising anyone of my intentions—I walked up the stairway, down the hallway, into our bedroom. There I knelt alone and confessed something like this:

Lord, I commit all of myself to you that I am able,
and I accept Jesus as your divine Son.

Without realizing it, I had been born again spiritually on the anniversary of the day I was born physically. My physical and spiritual birthdays were the same—but 44 years apart! For me there were no flashing lights or emotional outbursts at that time. But that birthday did mark the death of my old life and the beginning of a new life in Christ. Many things have happened since that time. Some of them have been pleasant and some have been difficult. I know now that when I surrendered my will to God to direct and control, I had to expect some changes to happen both to myself and to those around me. Sometimes those changes were painful. Yet, they were like a surgeon's scalpel, which hurt temporarily to correct a problem, but ultimately allowed me to live.

Although I didn't realize it at the time, the next few years were going to usher in a new direction in my life that was so far superior to my old self-controlled existence, I could never have dreamed it possible. For as soon as I tried to become fully committed in my Faith, the effect on my Marriage and Family, my Vocation, and all of life were dramatic and all for the good!

That brings us now to the most important question we will ask during this book or throughout our lives:

QUESTIONS

1. Have you fully "Surrendered" your life and will to Jesus and accepted Him as God and Lord over all you are and have?

2. If you have not fully Surrendered to Jesus, will you do it now?

3. If you have fully Surrendered to Him, describe what happened and how you can share your story with others.

A NEW DIRECTION
AGE 45–50

Therefore, if anyone is in Christ, he is a new creation;
the old has gone, the new has come!
(I Corinthians 5:17)

A mentor of mine once described surrender to Christ as one great big "Yes", followed by a lot of little "Uh Huhs". After I surrendered, it soon became apparent there were two other changes I needed to make:

> First: To go with God's people, instead of alone.
> Second: To go God's way, instead of my own.

Since our goal is to aid you in reflecting on your life and charting your own journey, let me describe some of the events and changes that unfolded during these next five years, and discoveries I made along the way.

First—To Go with God's People instead of "Alone"
Looking back I see several types of Christian fellowships that were very helpful:

1. Discipling
For some time I had been reading books, particularly by Elton Trueblood, about Christian fellowship. I was deeply impacted by his books *The Incendiary Fellowship* and *The Company of the Committed.* These small power-packed descriptions of Christian fellowship were intensely attractive to me. But I was still alone spiritually. I had family, professional, and social fellowship, but—

like so many men, as I would later discover—I had no other man with a kindred spirit to talk with and walk with in the difficult and eternal issues of life.

Finally, in desperation, I called a businessman I had met briefly when he and his family visited our church one Sunday. There was something about his presence and conversation (as confirmed to me by others who knew him) that made me believe he knew something about Christian fellowship that I wanted.

Looking back now I realize the hunger that was evident in my telephone request to him. I simply announced, "I have been reading about Christian fellowship, and I would like to know where I can find some." He didn't laugh or give me the name of a church to attend or a pastor to see or books to read. Instead, he graciously began to meet with me *himself* on a regular basis and to take me with him as he followed Christ.

The Bible says Jesus appointed twelve to "be with Him" (Mark 3:14). As helpful as studies and discipleship courses are, I have concluded the best description of "discipleship" is to follow Jesus' example, and the example I was given, i.e., "To take someone with you as you follow Christ." They learn as we learn; they laugh and cry as we laugh and cry; they risk as we risk. As one pastor concluded, "We are fellows in the same ship together; only some are a little further forward than others and they pass what they've received back to those who follow."

For the next three or four years, my new friend and I spent much time together studying, memorizing scripture, playing, and serving. Later, our relationship ripened into a mature lifelong friendship centered in Christ and our love for Him and for each other.

We need earthly parents to train us to think and act right in our physical lives, good bosses to train us competently and ethically in the early stages of our work life, and spiritual fathers to walk with us and help us to mature as we begin our life with Christ. As Paul wrote to the Corinthians,

Even though you have ten thousand guardians in Christ, you do not have many fathers, for in Christ Jesus I became your father through the gospel.
Therefore, I urge you to imitate me.
(1 Corinthians 4:15-16)

It is a rare privilege when God gives us such a person to guide and train us. And it is also a deep responsibility when God gives us a child, a working apprentice, or a spiritual child to walk with us and to "imitate" us. For that reason it is important that we also learn, for ourselves and for those who follow us, to heed carefully Paul's additional and sober warning:

Follow my example, **as I follow the example of Christ**.
(1 Corinthians 11:1; Emphasis supplied)

2. Mentoring

"Disciple" is a biblical term; "Mentor" is not. Rather, it comes from Greek mythology and was the name of Odysseus's trusted counselor. Although these terms are somewhat intermingled today, I believe there is a difference. In essence the first seems more like a father and the second, a grandfather. A discipler (a term coined for this concept although not commonly defined in the dictionary) yokes himself alongside us and walks closely with us for a period of time until we are trained. By contrast a mentor is one who counsels and advises us after we can walk alone but still need the counsel of an older and wiser head from time to time. I believe we need both disciplers and mentors.

I met my first spiritual mentor in the same way I obtained my first discipler. By asking! (See Matthew 7:7.) I have determined that those of us who want to receive all God has for us must sometimes humble ourselves and become spiritual beggars. We must cast all our pride and false egoism aside and ask!

Since I knew no older spiritual grandfather figure locally, I decided to call three authors whose writings had helped me in my quest. Two of them were so busy we couldn't make contact. However, my call to Dr. Elton Trueblood changed my life. A biography of him was sub-titled *Believer, Teacher, Friend.* And he was. At the time I contacted Dr. Trueblood he was about 70 years of age, and a well-known author and professor at a small Christian college. Although I was totally unknown to him, he welcomed my call and invited me to come for a visit. On the day I arrived, he had prepared a guest room for me. He spent the entire next day answering my questions and helping me sort out the direction my life should now take. I'll never forget his opening comment that was so unusual in our hurried, harried world. He smiled and said, "We have time! Isn't that wonderful? We have time!"

Mentors—like grandfathers—have time, and they are usually willing to share it with those who ask. It's a ministry I came to appreciate more and more over the years. We'll talk more about this topic as we discuss Generations III and IV.

3.Church, Parachurch, Small Groups, and One-on-One
I also found fellowship in our local church and from the Body of Christ at large. Fortunately, my pastor was sensitive to my search and suggested our family attend an InterVarsity Camp in Colorado. This experience opened the door to a parachurch world I never knew existed. Meeting in conferences, small groups, and one-on-one, evangelizing, teaching, and nurturing, these groups—such as Basic Youth Conflicts, The Navigators, Yokefellows, The Fellowship, Laity Lodge, and others—provided speakers and facilitators that were a spiritual banquet for me. Participation in such groups can begin to fill the ravenous hunger for God's word and desire for real fellowship that so often occur after we surrender ourselves to Jesus.

A constant theme I received from all those who discipled, mentored and taught me was the value of small-group relationships. I found these to be the essence of the church. Large gatherings are exciting and allow us to learn and worship, but it is only in small, more intimate settings, usually about 2 to 12 people, that we usually experience deep fellowship. Best of all, of course, is when we can talk and walk with our wives and physical families as brothers and sisters in the family of Christ!

And since our spiritual family also needs generational networking, I was repeatedly encouraged to have a more mature Christian, a Christian peer, and a less mature Christian in my life. I think that, too, is good advice.

In summary, if you want to experience all God has for you, I urge you to become vulnerable and participate regularly not only in regular church worship, but also in whatever other good Christian fellowship you can find—including home Bible studies, church or parachurch cell (small) groups, men's action groups, etc. When you do, I believe you will realize one day you are no longer alone.

Second—To Go God's Way Instead of My Own

After I surrendered to God, I was almost terrified that I might stray and get lost again. I recall praying many times, "Now that you've found me, Lord, don't let me go!" I purposed, therefore, to follow His way, not my own, in every area of life.

My first action after I surrendered my own life was to surrender control of my wife and my children. Why this was so difficult, I do not know. Probably pride. But it was soon apparent they were growing and prospering much better under His care, direction and control.

As new believers we often feel we ought to go someplace to follow Jesus. This was one of the first questions I posed to Dr. Trueblood when we met. After all, when we have a deep spiritual experience, aren't we to leave the world and enter "fulltime Christian service?"

His answer was a resounding, "No!" He encouraged me to return to my law practice and serve Christ there. I did, and what he suggested turned out to be the right decision for me. Because we are already trained in our secular career we can usually do it well and still have time for other ministry free of charge, particularly if we will lower our paid work load and modify our living standards accordingly.

Although I've never heard a sermon on this subject, it was the model urged by Paul to the Thessalonians:

For you yourselves know how you ought to **follow our example***.*
We were not idle when we were with you,
nor did we eat anyone's food without paying for it.
On the contrary, we worked night and day, laboring and toiling
so that we would not be burden to any of you.
We did this, not because we do not have the right to such help,
but in order **to make ourselves a model for you to follow***.*
(2 Thessalonians. 3:7-9; Emphasis supplied)

While Paul was entitled to be paid, and was sometimes supported by others, he seemed to see what a wonderful privilege it is to support ourselves while we minister free of charge! (Read, for example, I Corinthians 9). I am aware, of course, that this is an individual decision. But I believe we need to consider carefully the opportunities to serve, that may abound where we are, without the expense and lost time incurred in changing our location or our occupation.

I was deeply concerned, of course, that clients wanted a tough, no-holds-barred attorney, and I would lose business if people found out I was a true follower of Christ. Finally, my wife and I went to Colorado for a week so I could meditate and think through the problem. One afternoon on a hillside near Gunnison, Colorado, God gave me the answer. It came from the biblical story of Esther as she struggled with whether or not to reveal her Jewish identity to her pagan husband, the king, and ask him to save her people from being slaughtered. When I read her courageous example, I decided it was time for me, too, to take a stand. So I dedicated my law practice to God and said, like Esther,

And if I perish, I perish.
(Esther 4:16b)

The opportunity soon came to put this promise to the test. One day I heard a speaker ask, "Who would be the hardest three people for you to witness to?" I knew immediately, and they were all clients. His question continued to haunt me. A short time later I knew I was to respond to the challenge, regardless of the cost. With much fear and trembling, and being careful not to impose on work time, I found opportunities to give each of these three men a short summary of my spiritual journey. In retrospect, I don't know how much my speaking out helped these men. But it surely helped me. It made speaking out always seem easier after this difficult beginning.

Conclusion

It seems inherent that each generation must experience the stages of life for itself. Few of us will accept the lessons of history without testing them personally. I am convinced that most of us cannot skip the chapters of life. As I was once instructed, "You can't put a 60 year old head on a 20 year old body!" We usually need one chapter of life to understand the next chapter. But I don't believe it takes 75 years to learn most of life's major lessons. Therefore I urge you to be careful about trying to skip a chapter. But do try to surrender to Christ and answer life's great questions *early,* so you can then

Run with perseverance the race marked out for... [you].
(Hebrews 12:1b)

Perhaps the following questions will assist you as you or others in your family circle walk through this part of life and prepare to enter Generation III at age 50.

QUESTIONS

1. What "New Direction(s)" have you received from God--after fully surrendering to Him?

2. Is there a ministry or area of service where God may be calling you? If so, what is it? If not, should you begin to pray for Him to show what He has for you?

3. How can you have real Christian fellowship as you carry out God's directions? (Consider home Bible studies, parachurch ministries, small groups, and other opportunities.)

Generation III:
A Time to Help Others
to Learn and to Do
Age 50–75

...but at the age of fifty, they must retire
from their regular service and work no longer.
They may assist their brothers
in performing their duties at the Tent of Meeting,
but they themselves must not do the work.
This, then, is how you are to assign
the responsibilities of the Levites.
(Numbers 8: 25-26.)

Some say the Bible never speaks of retirement. It does as noted above. But the term as used here does not mean to stop our usefulness. Rather, we are now given the opportunity to change our activity to fit our new season of life. We can now stop focusing so much on our own development and production, and begin to assist others as they seek to discover and carry out God's plan for their lives.

These are the passing-it-on years, the early autumn of life. During this time we often move from being a parent to a grandparent. Although the first 25 years of "Learning" and the second 25 years of "Doing" are exciting, this third 25 years period, when we can "Help Others to Learn And to Do", can be one of the most fulfilling and satisfying parts of our lives. This is a time when God can increasingly multiply through others what He has been building in us during the past 50 years.

HARMONY
AGE 50–55

Finally, all of you, live in harmony with one another;
be sympathetic, love as brothers, be compassionate and humble.
Do not repay evil with evil or insult with insult, but with blessing,
because to this you were called so that you may inherit a blessing.
(1 Peter 3:8-9)

It was my 49th birthday and I was looking forward to completing Generation II shortly, and then moving into what someone had described to me as "The Fabulous Fifties". Our family was seated around the table just after completing our dinner, and I was feeling philosophical. "Some time ago," I said, "I heard of a man who was discussing the stages of life. He said that when he was a young boy, his greatest desire was for food. As he grew older, his desire changed to money, because that would allow him to buy all the food or other things he wanted. Still later his desire was for time, because he found that with time he could make the money to buy the things he wanted. But finally he concluded that the most important thing in life was relationships. That is where I am now," I announced as I surveyed all those nearest and dearest to me. "To me, relationships—you all—are the most important thing in life!" There was quiet for a moment. Then my 19 year old son, with a smile in his eyes, spoke up and said, "Can I have your money?"

Earlier in my life, relationships had not been so important to me. As a result I had found myself living in conflict much of the time. Now, I was beginning to experience one of the most rewarding blessings of my new life in Christ, as I gradually moved from an adversarial climate into a world with less discord and more harmony. My life was not perfect, of course, but it was much more enjoyable than the conflict-ridden environment I had previously known—and probably had helped to create.

The change manifested itself as I began to apply Biblical principles to our home, church, workplace and community; and, also, as the Holy Spirit became an integral part of my life. These events happened gradually over a period of many years, but I will try and review them at this time, and you can determine how they may help you in your journey.

Using the Bible as a Guide to Harmonious Relationships
I had begun studying the Bible regularly—not just for academic study, but because I was desperate for guidance about how to live my life with others. As I read, I was increasingly drawn to the book of Ephesians. I began to see that God had laid out for us a guide for relationships: first with him, then with other believers, husband and wife, parent and child, employer and employee, and, finally, even instructions for our struggle against the devil. As I read, studied, meditated, and prayed about these and other similar scriptures, I began to see God's plan was reconciliation—not conflict. And His method was for us to *complete* each other, rather than to *compete against* each other. Following God's plan for relationships, laid out in Ephesians and elsewhere in the Bible, began to bring some harmony and peace into my life.

I saw that God has given us roles in the various institutions in which he has placed us. When I accepted my role as a man, husband, father, employer, citizen, etc., and carried out the Biblical responsibilities in each area—while helping others find and carry out their Biblical roles—I found harmony, rather than discord, in more and more of my relationships. In order to aid you in your journey, let me discuss some areas where I tried to apply these principles.

The Workplace

Most of my law practice consisted of representing management in labor-relations matters, particularly those involving unions. For years I had watched the battles of litigation, negotiations and bitter—sometimes violent—strikes that often left deep scars. It was hard not to become personally involved. At one point we had our own office bombed.

Finally I decided there had to be a better way. For several months I analyzed 25 or 30 union disputes we had handled. Each night after work, I would sit in our basement reviewing these cases to determine, "What is causing such strife in the workplace?" I had thought that the issue would be about money. But as the cases gradually unfolded, I found that the issue was really about relationships, and that we usually fought about the money after the relationships were broken. I found there were four common problems and four scriptural antidotes:

Problem	Antidote
Faulty Supervision	Servant Leadership
Change	Communication
Incompetence	Discipline (as in "disciple")
Divided Houses	Security

As these principles were amplified, and then taught and applied by management, we began to see relationships strengthened and discord minimized. Conflict was never completely eliminated, since we are sinful people, but environments were changed for the better. I gradually began to see the validity of Dr. Trueblood's advice to me to return to my normal life, so that Jesus and His truths could be carried into my everyday surroundings and sphere of influence. Truth is truth. We don't have to quote chapter and verse in order to see it work.

The principles were presented in seminars and training sessions under the title, *Harmony in the Workplace.* Later, small booklets were prepared and sent to some of our clients and to others I thought might have an interest. Again, the response was positive. I encourage you that God does provide ways for us to be used by Him in our workplace, if we rely upon Him and work in natural, rather than contrived ways. *And always for the benefit of those we are attempting to serve.*

Marriage

As I studied these issues, I discovered the same basic relationship problems happened in all four institutions i.e. Family, Church, Workplace and Government. For example, as I studied the Biblical roles of Husband and Wife, I found a similar scriptural pattern unfolding for harmony in our marriages, which have also seen much discord in recent years. As these principles, using scripture and the Spirit as our guide and Jesus as the center of our relationships were amplified and applied in my own life and then in the lives of others, discord seemed to decrease and harmony increased.

I encourage you that we can have more harmony in all our institutions, which will bless us and those who follow us in life, if we follow Jesus and His Word rather than the ever changing precepts of the world.

Asking for the Holy Spirit

Another key factor in creating harmony was when I identified and began using my spiritual gifts and recognized the spiritual gifts of others. I'm not sure when I first became spiritually aware of Luke 11:13. This passage comes at the end of one of Jesus' great teachings on prayer, particularly relating to our need to ask. Jesus concludes the instruction with this challenge:

If you then, though you are evil, know how to give good
gifts to your children, how much more will your Father in heaven
give the Holy Spirit to those who ask him!
(Emphasis supplied)

I realize there is great disagreement among genuine believers over the role of the Holy Spirit, including when and how He enters our lives and how He manifests Himself. I cannot answer these issues, but I can tell you what I found as I searched and asked.

I began to talk with God and said in essence, "God, if there is more—if the Holy Spirit is to be involved in my life—I want to have it. I want to be filled with the Holy Spirit." I read a number of accounts about Holy Spirit experiences of people who had been greatly used by God. I found it was often a very emotional encounter as well as a turning point in their lives.

My own experience was much the same. I was driving alone on the Kansas Turnpike on my way to a labor-relations session of some kind. It was my custom to use these drives for prayer and scripture memory. Suddenly, and without warning, I felt overpowered with emotion. It was a life-changing experience. I cannot explain it. I do not know if it is to happen to everyone. *I do know the scripture says we are to ask!*

Gifts of the Holy Spirit

I also found another key factor in building harmony in my relationships was to learn to identify and then understand my spiritual gift(s) and the spiritual gifts of others with whom I was to be in tune. I Corinthians 12-14, Ephesians 4, Romans 12 and 1 Peter 4:10-11 together with several speakers and writers, were all very helpful.

When it appeared likely that I had the gift of mercy, I rebelled. I felt it might destroy my career. Who would want a lawyer, especially one involved in labor relations, to have such a sensitive gift? Yet when I finally accepted God's gracious gift, I found it was a perfect fit—as long as I was not trying to win at all costs but rather to bring about lasting and healthy long-term relationships by eliminating discord and bringing a spirit of reconciliation and harmony into the workplace.

It is tempting, of course, to magnify the value of our gift over others. We can also be tempted to embezzle our gifts for our own personal power, pleasure, and profit, rather than using them to glorify God and to bless others. Both can be disastrous.

Identifying and using these spiritual gifts can also build stronger marriages. Our wives are somewhat puzzling to us simply because they are women. Dear, dear women, but still the opposite gender. But I have found there can also be a struggle because spouses often have different spiritual gifts. I believe there is a natural tension among the gifts in marriage as well as in other institutions. But once we understand our own gift(s) and the gift(s) of our wife, we can operate more efficiently as one, and we can also appreciate the value the other one brings to us and to our families.

This same tension among spiritual gifts also seems to be present in the church. Rulers may seem harsh to those with the gift of mercy; and those with mercy seem weak and indecisive to those gifted in ruling. But each has a valuable part to play. When we listen to the Holy Spirit speaking through our own gifts—and also through the gifts of others around us—we can stop playing a solo, or someone else's instrument, and begin to be a part of an orchestra of God producing harmony and making the Body of Christ more effective, attractive, and enjoyable.

Fruit of the Spirit

In Galatians 5:16–26 Paul describes the eternal conflict between our sinful nature and God's Holy Spirit. He urges us to "live by the Spirit." I have found that when we do this, our lives increasingly reflect the "fruit of the Spirit" including "love," "joy," and "peace" rather than "discord," dissension," "factions," and the other painful fruit of our old sinful nature.

Knowing the Holy Spirit as a Person

I had slowly realized God the Father was becoming closer and more personal as I viewed Him as *my* Father. And the Messiah (Christ) was becoming increasingly real as I gradually accepted the fact that I was following a Person, not just a creed, and that I could speak lovingly to Him as "Jesus" or "*my* Lord". But the Holy Spirit had remained "*The* Holy Spirit" in my mind. He never seemed close or personal, but rather mysterious and vague like a vapor. Since this Spirit is *my* Counselor, *my* Comforter, and *my* Teacher, I wanted a more intimate and personal relationship with Him. I decided, therefore, to speak to Him more often, and by name, and to remove the "the" when I addressed Him. It was helpful. Somehow He (like "my Father" and "Jesus, my Lord") has become more personal to me as I have spoken directly with Him and addressed Him as a Person (i.e. "Holy Spirit") rather than as a title (i.e. "The Holy Spirit"). Perhaps this will help you, too.

Let's look now at some questions that may be of some aid to you as you think through these issues. If you have not already done so, you may want to chart your journey to date, and perhaps the journeys of others in your family, on the Life Line at the end of the book, as you reflect on this opening chapter of Generation III.

QUESTIONS

1. What blessing (such as "Harmony") do you feel called to bring into the world(s) around you?

2. Think about any relationships where there is discord. What can you do to bring about reconciliation?

3. What spiritual gift(s) have you been given to carry out God's will for your life?

REACHING OUT
AGE 55–60

But you will receive power when the Holy Spirit comes on you;
and you will be my witnesses in Jerusalem,
and in all Judea and Samaria, and to the ends of the earth.
(Acts 1:8)

By age 55, I was agreeing that the decade of the Fifties usually has some good years. For most of us, our children are maturing, completing their education, and leaving home for careers and families of their own. This is a bittersweet time. On the one hand, we realize that a very important part of our life is drawing to a close, and we will deeply miss the everyday presence of our children, with their laughter and fun, mixed with challenges and crises. However, on the other hand, this new period often opens up great new opportunities. As one homespun "philosopher" quipped, "Life begins when the ole dog dies and the children leave home!"

After many years of intense responsibilities, the pressure seems to be reducing. If the years have treated us reasonably well, we often have more discretionary time and money. We become aware that we have the liberty to stretch out into some new experiences. The question is, *"What shall we do with our new freedom?"* You will have to make that decision for yourself, but many find this is a time for increased opportunities to witness for Christ.

Acts 1:8 reminds us that we are to start witnessing at home (our Jerusalem), and then reach out into the surrounding areas (Judea and Samaria), and finally to the *"ends of the earth."* As we move into our middle years, we often have increased opportunities and freedom to speak not only to a larger family, but also to a larger audience in our workplace, church, and community. As a result we need to become prepared and then let God use us as His spokesman when the opportunities arise. Here is some more information that may help.

What Is a "Witness"?

The term "witness" is both a noun and a verb. Just as we "love" (verb) with "love" (noun), so are we able "*to* witness" (verb) because we have become "*a* witness" (noun). A witness sees or hears something and then tells what he or she has seen or heard. In court, most facts are proven by the testimony of witnesses, and usually only those can testify who have personally observed the fact(s) in issue.

As we observe others, we not only listen to what they say, we also watch to see what they are and what they do. Others do the same thing with us. *In order to be credible, our character and our conduct must match our words.* When John's disciples asked Jesus if he was "the one who was to come," he replied,

> ... *Go back and report to John what you hear and see:*
> *The blind receive sight, the lame walk,*
> *those who have leprosy are cured,*
> *the deaf hear, the dead are raised,*
> *and the good news is preached to the poor.*
> (Matthew. 11:3-5b)

To prove His authority, Jesus recounted *five* things he *did* and only *one* thing He *said*. This is not a bad ratio for us today. As

I heard one of Jesus' followers (who probably had the gift of service) comment, "Go and spread the gospel and, if you have to, use words!" (See also Colossians 4:2–6, especially verse 4.)

Witnesses in the Bible
The Bible contains numerous accounts of men and women who saw and/or heard God through visions, dreams, dramatic experiences, or "a still small voice." In the Old Testament, people such as Abraham, Elijah, Samuel, Job, and the prophets all encountered God, believed, and were blessed for eternity. Each of them, in turn, then became a witness to others—including our generation—of what they had seen and heard so that we, too, might draw closer to God.

The Four Accounts of the Gospel and the Book of Acts in the New Testament contain the accounts of dozens of witnesses who met Jesus personally, or through His Spirit. These books of the Bible then tell what happened when those who encountered Jesus believed and turned and followed Him; or when they refused to believe and turned away from Him. For example, the Gospel of John records over 30 individuals or groups who encountered Jesus. Many believed and followed Him; others refused to believe and went on their way. Without exception, those who truly believed and followed Him walked into joy and fullness of life, although often mixed with pain and problems; and those who turned away missed the blessings.

Why Do *We* Witness?
The same principle appears to be true today. Some people regret that they have never met Jesus or that they have met him and turned away. But I've never met anyone *who truly met*

Jesus and decided to follow Him who regretted their decision! And, because the blessings that flow from this experience are so great, it usually causes us to want to share it with others!

We seem to be like Peter and John when those in authority sought to silence them:

> *Then they called them in again and commanded them*
> *not to speak or teach at all in the name of Jesus.*
> *But Peter and John replied,*
> *"Judge for yourselves whether it is right in God's sight*
> *to obey you rather than God.*
> *For we cannot help speaking about what we have seen and heard."*
> (Acts 4:18–20)

I believe those who have decided to follow Jesus become His witnesses not merely because He commanded it, but also because their hearts sometimes feel as if they will burst if they don't share the "Good News" (Gospel). For what could be more exciting and gratifying than to meet Someone who forgives our sins, cleans us up, and gives us the power to walk with Him and His family in joy and a sense of purpose for eternity?

Preparing Our Testimony
For whatever reason, God has not chosen to meet most of us through dramatic visions, dreams or supernatural events. Instead we usually meet Him through the witness of ordinary men and women who love Jesus and us so much they want to introduce us to the One who has meant so much to them. All our stories are different, yet the same. Each of us has traveled our own unique way, met Him somewhere along the road, and then followed

Him on our own personal journey. Yet every personal testimony seems to be made up of the same Biblical elements:

- God loved me and created me.
- I went my own way and became lost.
- People began to tell me about a man named Jesus who had shown them "the way," and they wanted to share the "good news" with me.
- One day I met Jesus and believed He was God.
- He invited me to follow Him, and I accepted.
- Since I turned and followed Him, the world has turned right side up.
- The way is often hard, but now I feel secure in His love and care.
- Because God loves me, I now have a heart for others.
- Now I want to tell you about Jesus and invite you to meet him.
- I hope you, too, will believe and follow Him so we can all be together for eternity.
  The Bible says,

Always be prepared to give an answer to everyone who asks you to give the reason
for the hope that you have. But do this with gentleness and respect...
(1 Peter 3:15b)

One of the best scriptural models of a concise, powerful testimony by a witness is that given by Paul as recorded in Acts 26. It sets forth his life before Christ (verses 1–11), his encounter with Christ (verses 12–18), what happened after he met Christ (verses 19–23), and his desire for his listeners to follow Christ (verses 24–29). Paul's testimony takes place while he is on trial for his life and only takes about five minutes to recount!

It is important for each of us to prepare *our* testimony so *we* can be a witness for Jesus when the occasion arises. I procrastinated, but one afternoon I followed the suggestion of a more mature Christian friend and wrote down my story. That evening I was asked for the first time to share my spiritual journey! I believe God wants us to "be prepared" *before* He calls us to witness for Him.

Being *His* Witness

Jesus said, "You will be *my* witnesses." Therefore, if we want to be *His* witness, *He* should be the focal point of our comments, rather than our other interests or ourselves. And the key to each testimony is our meeting with Christ and what has happened as a result. As one listener asked, "What difference has it made in your life?"

When seekers hear witness after witness—both in scripture and today—describe their meeting with Jesus and what then happened in their lives, it causes the listener to see more clearly and to want to follow Him. When we keep our testimony and our eyes focused on Jesus, He will increase, we will decrease, and others will join in surrendering and following Him.

Expanding Our Horizon

While my witnessing began in my Jerusalem (i.e., my home, family, church, and workplace) it soon moved out to my Judea and Samaria, and even to other parts of the world. Visits to other homes, families, churches, and communities became an important part of my life. I encourage you that you will gain untold strength and renewed spiritual vigor as you go out to witness for Jesus in other locations and cultures.

I found I needed to cross age, racial, doctrinal, and economic boundaries as well as visiting others' geographic locations. How we profit as we begin to see how wide and deep God's family really is! As we move out, we begin to center our faith more on Jesus, His Father and His Spirit, and are bound less and less by a place, an organization or a tradition. Whether we work, play, or eat, whether we kneel, raise our hands, clap, sing, dance, or use an organ or a guitar, whether we are with old people, excited youngsters, or small children, in a beautiful sanctuary, outdoors, or the workplace, whether we are with those of our own color and economic background or not is all secondary. Our principle assignment is simply to love God and the people He puts in our path.

God created us all. As we mature, He often graciously allows us to scatter beyond our own geographic, cultural, economic, racial and traditional boundaries and to be His witnesses whenever and wherever we are called.

Now we come again to a time when you can reflect personally and determine how this period of life may apply to you.

QUESTIONS

1. Where and how is God calling you to "Reach Out" for Him?

2. In order to be prepared when God calls you to speak (witness) for Him,
a) Describe your life before you met Jesus.

b) Describe your first meeting with Jesus.

c) Describe your life since meeting Jesus.

HARVEST TIME
AGE 60–65

Keep falsehood and lies far from me; give me neither poverty nor riches,
but give me only my daily bread. Otherwise, I may have too
much and disown you
and say, "Who is the Lord?" Or I may become poor and steal,
and so dishonor the name of my God.
(Proverbs 30:8-9)

As we reach our 60's many of us begin to feel the chill of the autumn of our life. Our children are usually grown and we see our work life coming to an end soon. It seems to be a time for reflection about the past and for decisions to be made for the future.

Reaping What We've Sown
A dear woman I know calls our 60s, "The Harvest Time." The Bible says it this way:

> *Do not be deceived: God cannot be mocked.*
> *A man reaps what he sows.*
> (Galatians 6:7)

What we have believed and done in our earlier years is now coming to fruition—both good and bad. Most of us probably don't think early enough or strongly enough about what we will someday harvest. How I applaud the example of one man who often quoted this valuable rule as he was making decisions during his younger years: "I want to live my life so when I look back at age 60, I'll like what I see."

Each of us will have our own list of fruit we consider important as we come to our harvest time in life. Here are a few areas that seem important to me. Perhaps they will be helpful to you as you think about this issue:

1. <u>Character</u>—Whether we are yielding to our sinful nature or walking with God's Spirit will become increasingly apparent as we age. I decided I wanted to end up "a sweet old guy" and not "an angry, bitter old man."

2. <u>Families</u>—While each person is responsible for accepting or rejecting his own sinful nature or Jesus, it is also apparent that we see much of the harvest of our own lives in the character and conduct of our children, grandchildren, and others who follow us in life.

3. <u>Health</u>—A noted physician made a memorable talk to our local Prayer Breakfast several years ago. He listed five major contributors to death in men, all of which are primarily under an individual's control: "alcohol, tobacco, diet, exercise, and seat belts!" Both the positive and negative aspects of these factors became increasingly apparent as I reached my 60's.

4. <u>Wealth</u>—If we have been reasonably diligent with our money and have not had debilitating illnesses or personal tragedies, many of us will be able to support ourselves without working for pay during our later years. This freedom, or lack of it, can play a major part in the decisions we make about our future.

5. <u>Work</u>—The value attached to our work becomes a visible part of the harvest we see as we look back over our lives.

6. Wisdom—If we want to have wisdom in our later years to pass on to those who follow, we can't wait until we retire. It requires long years of walking closely with Jesus, His Spirit, His Word and His people.

How Much Is Enough?

As I reviewed my life at age 60, I realized I also needed to realign my course for the future: What should I stop? What should I continue? And what should I begin?

I mentioned earlier two provocative questions I was asked by a friend's mother at a dinner party we were attending. We discussed the first question ("What is your definition of success?") in the earlier chapter, *Striving for Success*. But the second question was very timely for me when it was asked, because it was one of the issues with which I was then wrestling. Although I was already in my 60's, the woman and her husband were in their 80's, so I listened attentively. They had been married over 60 years and I respected their experience and wisdom. She put the question simply and bluntly: "One decision you must make in life," I was told, "is how much is enough?" How much money? How much house? How many children? How much is enough—of everything?

As I thought about this issue, I determined there were some areas where I had enough. I decided, therefore:

1. No more trial work. Courtroom action is a game for young men or old lions. I decided I was neither.

2. No more firm management. Those who are following cannot take their rightful place of leadership until we get out of the way.

3. <u>No more acquisition of capital</u>. We all trade our lives for something. I decided that trading any more of my life for extra money wasn't a wise exchange.

4. <u>Setting A Time Table</u>. I also decided, and announced to my partners, that at age 65 I would sell my interest in the firm and go "of counsel", i.e., be a lawyer at large working only on a case by case basis, and retire at age 70. At first the other lawyers resisted my decision. But when I asked again about six months later, one responded, "It's the best decision you ever made!" (Which was a little *too* enthusiastic!)

I do not know what decision you will or should make. But I do believe we should review our lives periodically and ask the question, "How much is enough for me at this stage in my life?"

Crisis Point Number Three

I found that the first three generations were following a general pattern. Each usually began with about ten good (calm) years, followed by ten or so rocky years—often including a crisis—and ending with about five years of exciting change as we set our direction for the next 25 year chapter.

Thus, in Generation I, age 1-10 was usually stable; age 10-20 was often full of turmoil as we faced Crisis Number One in our "Traumatic Teens"; and age 20-25 typically saw us deciding what we believed, who we would marry, and what our life work would be.

Generation II seemed to repeat the process: age 25-35 was usually on course and productive with new jobs and new families; age 35-45 often saw us re-evaluating our faith, our marriage and our vocation as we walked, or bounced, through our mid-life crisis; and age 45-50 usually found us with renewed confidence setting our direction for the mature part of life.

Now Generation III seemed to be following the same pattern. As I looked at my life and the lives of others, age 50-60 were usually golden years as our work expanded and our grandchildren began to bless our lives; but the "Sober Sixties" seemed destined to be another decade of change and even turmoil. We now saw our youthfulness and usefulness fading away and we wondered how to face these final years of physical and sometimes financial, mental or even marital decline.

Unfortunately, most of us get our sense of worth from what we do rather than whose we are. Thus, when our work life threatens to come to an end we sometimes panic if we are not confident of our status as children of God. I have heard men at this stage say repeatedly, in effect, "It isn't fun anymore. It's all changing, and I feel more and more out of step. I've done my job long enough." Some then add, "But I'm afraid to retire. I don't know what I'd do!"

The world tells us that our worth *is* bound up in our youthfulness and usefulness. As both of these fade, so can our self-esteem. And as that is happening, another difficult transition often occurs, and our life journey may take another downward swing like this:

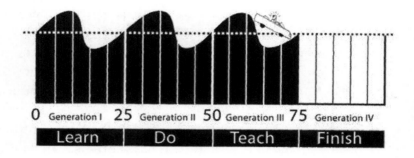

0	Generation I	25	Generation II	50	Generation III	75	Generation IV
Learn		Do		Teach		Finish	

This is not a new view. In chapter 27 of Leviticus, written 3500 years ago, God Himself set forth the following equivalent values for redeeming males dedicated to Him:

Age 5–20	—	20 Shekels
Age 20–60	—	50 Shekels
Age 60 and over	—	15 Shekels

We know, of course, that in God's eyes we all have the same *eternal* value regardless of our age or other characteristics. However, the humbling fact is that from a physical standpoint, even God seems to be saying that we are worth more at 16 or even 6 than we are at 60! This must be the *original* "Senior Discount!"

It is a reality of life that we wear out! We can sometimes hold it off for awhile, but ultimately our physical, and sometimes mental, energies and capabilities decline with age.

Our scary task now is to make the transition to a new, more sedate role in life and still maintain our sense of worth and eternal usefulness.

A Look at the Future

Much has been written and discussed about the unrealized potential of healthy retirees who now have time to help others as unpaid volunteers. There *is* much excellent volunteer work being done by seniors. However, it seems that most of us will major in retirement doing what was a minor during our working lives. In essence, our avocation before retirement often becomes our vocation after retirement—whether it's working with our investments, teaching Bible studies, or playing golf. We don't seem to change to something new, as much as we expand what we were already doing. Thus, if you want to be serving the Lord in retirement, don't wait. Begin now to serve Him where you are. Then you will be prepared and in motion to continue with Him when retirement comes.

My own release and reassignment came a few months before my 65th birthday. After many months of asking for direction, I was awakened early one morning with a sense of peace and a voice saying, "Your assignment for the rest of your life is simply to love people and to love me."

When I asked, it was repeated. I was overwhelmed with the simplicity of it. So basic! I guess that is really the full time, lifetime, job given to us all when we decide to follow Jesus.

Now it's your opportunity to take a look at the issues being raised by this time period of life and see how you believe they may apply to you and your family circle. For starters I have set forth the following question that may help.

QUESTIONS

"How much is enough" for you in every area of life?

Home:

Money:

Work:

Recreation and Travel:

Family and Friends:

Church:

Giving:

Other:

PASSING THE BATON
AGE 65–70

Then the Lord replied: "Write down the revelation
and make it plain on tablets so that a herald may run with it. "
(Habakkuk 2:2)

Not long before I retired, an older physician offered me some advice. "Don't work too long," he said. When I inquired about his comment, he answered with a story. It seemed that an older surgeon wanted to work as long as possible, but he was concerned about making an error in the closing years of his career. So he asked his long-time assistant to tell him if she saw evidence it was time for him to retire. Finally the time arrived and the assistant— reluctantly, I'm sure—did as she had been instructed. My friend then asked me, "Do you know what her boss did when she told him it was time? He fired her!" My friend then concluded, "The point is, none of us thinks it's time for us!"

Retirement
I do not know when the right time is for you to retire—if ever. Samuel was probably about 65 years old when he gave up his position as Judge over Israel. (See New International Version Study Bible note on 1 Samuel 8:1.) But, in Exodus 7:7, we read that Moses was 80 when he *began* to lead the Israelites out of Egypt. However, his life may not have been normative, since he also wrote Psalm 90:10a, which says,

The length of our days is seventy years—
or eighty if we have the strength...

But I do sense there is some appropriate time for us to consider making a change as we complete Generation III and prepare to enter Generation IV.

Some, particularly those who did not enjoy their jobs, can't seem to wait to retire. Their work has become a burden, so the sooner the better! As one proposed retirement plan used to boast, "Fifty and out!" Others apparently take retirement in stride. When it's time, it's time, and they move on willingly and contentedly.

Still others, particularly those who have enjoyed or received their sense of value from their work, often appear reluctant to stop. They may not leave until poor health, stress, or company pressures or inducements force them out.

If we listen, I believe God has a way of telling us when, and if, it's time. Sometimes it's loss of desire, loss of competence, or simply loss of energy to keep up with younger coworkers. When these indicators are accompanied by subtle—or so people think— inquires asking, "When are you going to retire?" we begin to realize our full-time work life is probably coming to an end.

I have heard some caution, "Don't retire, or you will stagnate and die." Perhaps that is a concern for some. But the stress of travel, competition, and conflict made me more concerned that I might die if I didn't retire! In fact, I believe I grew healthier and felt better after I retired than at age 65 when I made the change. All these points simply illustrate that this is an individual decision, but I believe it is a decision that should be faced and not ignored.

Whatever the timing, we have to deal with the stigma attached to the term "retirement." It is an unfortunate word. It describes something we are *not*. Just as widows no longer have husbands, and orphans no longer have parents, so most folks seem to believe retirees no longer have any job that makes a significant contribution to society. As a result, retirement causes us to reevaluate our lives— particularly when we are increasingly asked, "So now that you're retired, what do you do with your time?"

Beware of a Vacuum

I thought it would be difficult to make the break from full-time law practice, but I didn't know how difficult. In preparation, I wrote to several men in my age group to ask them to join me in walking through these years together. All of them loved the Lord, were devoted family men, and had been principals or in charge of a work group. We represented several branches of the church. I told them I needed help, and this was an "S.O.S." I wanted to meet regularly with some "Sold-out Seniors for Christ" to help and encourage one another as we retired, semi-retired, or kept going full pace as the case might be. Eight of us began meeting regularly, and it helped me immeasurably.

As the years have progressed, I have become increasingly aware how essential it is that we have fellowship—particularly in the difficult transitions of life. It is not easy to watch age, illness, and death take its toll among our family and friends. But having some like-minded friends going through the journey with us is certainly helpful.

Spiritually, this was a difficult time for me. I learned the danger of sweeping out the old, but not having my heart and mind filled with something new. I know now never to leave a vacuum. Having a direction for the future is critical, or the devil may move in with all sorts of doubts and dark thoughts as he did in my case. (See Luke 11:24–26.) So I encourage you to have a plan for what you are moving *to* and not just what you are retiring *from*!

Vocation

For many years I did not sufficiently appreciate the difference between our vocation and our job or profession. The world interchanges these terms and so did I. Gradually, however, I began to see that our vocation—or what I sometimes refer to as our "voca," as in "vocal"—is actually our "calling" from God. By contrast I believe our job or profession is the way we financially support ourselves, and *one* place where we carry out our vocations. Thus, if my *calling* is to *bring harmony* then I do that in my job or profession, but I also do it at home, at church, and in the community. It's much like the distinction between "transportation" and "railroads" or "airlines." The latter two are simply tools to help accomplish the former. So, too, jobs and professions, I believe, are merely tools to help us carry out the broader calling we receive from God.

The Apostle, Paul, understood this distinction. Sometimes he supported himself as a tentmaker. (See Acts 18:3 and 2 Thessalonians 3:7–10.) Sometimes he was supported by other churches, as in 2 Corinthians 11:8. And sometimes he was supported by the state—as a prisoner! (See 1 Corinthians 11:23.) The *method* of financial support—which today we would refer to as his job or profession—often changed, but the message of the gospel never varied as he carried out his calling from God described in Acts 26:17–18:

I will rescue you from your own people and from the Gentiles.
I am sending you to them to open their eyes and turn them from
darkness to light,
and from the power of Satan to God,
so that they may receive forgiveness of sins
and a place among those who are sanctified by faith in me.

Regardless of his job or method of support, Paul never wavered from this original calling from God. (See Acts 26:19–29 and Colossians 1:24–29.)

Like Paul, we are to carry out the commission or calling God gives to us, regardless of circumstances. Age, health, or other factors may cause us to retire from our job or our profession— but not from our vocation. We are still to be about God's business, in whatever way he calls us to serve, even though we may now be financially supported by pensions or savings rather than by salaries or other earned income.

I believe our call, or at least the emphasis of our call, may change as we move through life. But I don't think we abolish or abandon what we were doing as much as we build on it. The work we have done at each stage of life has been important in its time. But now as we retire, we have the opportunity to build on our early years and experiences to complete the final work God has for us in these later years. As one wise older man told me, "Don't do something entirely new after you retire; instead, hone what you worked on earlier." Like Peter, we don't stop being fishermen; rather, we can now concentrate on being fishers of *men*, without having also to concern ourselves with catching *fish*! (See Luke 5:1–11.)

Passing On Our Vision

I don't know how God will use you in these later years. But I believe He has a unique plan for *all* the days of our lives; and that part of that plan for this period may include passing on to others what He has taught us over the years. Psalm 71:18 says it this way:

> *Even when I am old and gray, do not forsake me, O God,*
> *till I declare your power to the next generation,*
> *your might to all who are to come.*

My particular urge was to bridge the gap that I saw between God's teachings and the way that I, and others, were living our everyday lives. This became my goal; never fully reached, but at least a goal for these later years. During these five years (age 65-70), I taught and wrote about many of the subjects I had been studying and attempting to apply and then pass on to others during the previous years. One booklet I felt particularly appropriate for our grandchildren, I placed in our lock-box with a personal note, for delivery to each one as they reached age 21.

Now I am consolidating many of the booklets I have been writing over the years into books such as this one so they can be available to my children, their children, and their children (i.e., to the fourth generation).

Again, let me emphasize, I don't know your vision, nor to whom you are to pass it on. But I sincerely believe God will make it clear to you as you seek His guidance and walk with Him. Here are some questions that may aid you in your quest.

QUESTIONS

1. What is your "Vision"—and to whom will you pass it on?

2. What do you see as the relationship between your job, your vocation, and retirement?

3. What Christian friends in your age group could form a support group with you when you are transitioning into a new chapter of life?

BE READY
AGE 70–75

Therefore keep watch, because you do not know on what day your Lord will come...So you also must be ready, because the Son of Man will come at an hour when you do not expect him.
(Matthew 24:42, 44)

Finishing well is often the hardest part of a race, a project or a life. As we come to the last five years of Generation III and prepare to enter Generation IV at about age 75, many of us realize we are tiring and wearing out. If we are to finish well in our life race, we sense we need to make some preparations for these final years. Here are some of the items I considered that may help you as you think about this period of life:

- How does my life fit in history?
- What are some of the challenges that lie ahead in Generation IV?
- What specific action shall we take to prepare for Generation IV?

How Does My Life Fit in History?
As we move through Generation III (Age 50-75) we continue to expand our view of time. During these years we seem to be stirred by a broader view of history and the part we play in it. As we look backward, our roots become increasingly important, and we often start to work on our genealogy and family history. Even more importantly, we often also look ahead and consider what we can, and should, pass on to those who follow. I found I was no

exception as I began just before age 70 to prepare the material that became the essence of this book.

No longer do we see time as beginning when we are born and ending when we die. Instead we become increasingly aware that God is directing *all* history, and that our life, the lives of those who have gone before us, and the lives of those who come after us are all tied together in a continuum. We are all affected by the past, and we all affect not only the present but, also, the future.

Interestingly, history (His Story as recorded in the Bible and the church) seems to follow a rather methodical pattern—like many of our lives—and to be marked by a similar rollercoaster of ups and downs, peaks and valleys. I believe it looks like this.

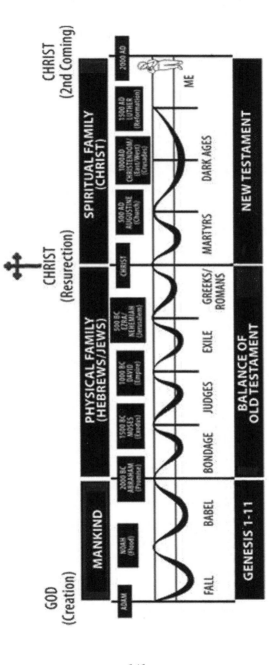

It is difficult to see either a monumental peak or valley since the Reformation in AD 1500. But if we continue these 500 year cycles, it seems likely we are on the threshold of a *very* historic time around the year AD 2000. Many seem to have a sense of anticipation, or foreboding, almost as if we were feeling the birth pangs of an event about to occur. The end of the cold war, the fragmentation of historic institutions, and the explosion of technology have left us unsettled. For the first time in history, computer networking, globalization, and the intertwining of economies all seem to point to the possibility of a new one-world era.

For those who are drawn to eschatology, this may herald the end times spoken of so graphically by Daniel (in the Book of Daniel) and by Jesus (e.g., Matthew 24). For some, such a series of events point to unlimited new opportunities. And for others it portends terrible chaos and difficulties as we go through the coming years.

I am not a prophet. But I sense we are moving into a time of political, economic and social change greater than we have seen for 500 years—perhaps greater than we have ever known. Therefore, I believe we need to be prepared spiritually and physically! To me this means being sure we are fully surrendered and ready to meet Jesus, whether He comes to earth or calls us Home. We also need to be ready to weather any storms that may come and to help others spiritually and physically if chaotic times do occur during our lifetime.

As we view the broad historical picture of what God has done over the centuries, and what He may be about to do now, it makes us realize just how small we are in God's total plan. Each of us *is* important and significant to God (e.g. Psalm 8:4-8). But when we finally see ourselves in relation to Him, we must conclude, like Job

> *Surely I spoke of things I did not understand,*
> *things too wonderful for me to know...*
> *My ears had heard of you*
> *but now my eyes have seen you.*
> *Therefore I despise myself and repent in dust and ashes.*
>
> (Job 42:3b, 5–6)

As we increasingly see the magnitude of God's plan, we no longer strive to hold so tightly to our own power and possessions and our few years in history. Maturity seems to bring with it a willingness to let God have his way. Instead of wanting an epitaph centered on ourselves, mature believers often look for ways for God to receive the glory and recognition. Many are not only willing, but increasingly desire, that Jesus might increase and they might decrease.

Life is not a meaningless circle. God created us and despite our rebellion He is calling each generation to return and enjoy Him throughout our lives and into all eternity. I believe this little poem summarizes it well:

> *God knows where we're going,*
> *And God knows where we've been.*
> *God has made eternal plans for us,*
> *That will never end.*

History's on a countdown,
It isn't just a whim;
For God knows where we're going,
And God know where we've been.

The Bible makes it clear that God has a plan for all creation, and that includes a plan for each of us. As He says in Jeremiah 29:11:

"For I know the plans I have for you," declares the LORD,
"plans to prosper you and not to harm you,
plans to give you hope and a future."

As a result we can now begin to relax and watch with interest— and even with some contentment—to see what God intends to do through this last generation of our lives.

What Are Some of the Challenges That Lie Ahead in Generation IV?

Moses, in his final song at the end of Deuteronomy, concluded:

Remember the days of old; consider the generations long past.
Ask your father and he will tell you,
your elders, and they will explain to you.
(Deuteronomy 32:7)

As I approached my 70th birthday, I decided it was time for me, also, to visit with someone who had already lived through some of the years up ahead. I called a man I respected who was about ten years my senior and said, "I would like to come down and talk with you about the 70's." He agreed, and we set the date.

I asked one of our teenage grandsons to go along, for the fellowship and also for what he might learn. I said, "Come on, and you can learn what you need to know for your 70's." I had to smile at his honest reply, "But, Grandpa, I don't think I'll remember!" However, he agreed to go anyway. We flew down to our host's city and met with him for about two or three hours. Here's what we heard.

First—Learn to manage *deterioration*. All our lives have been spent managing growth in our families, our finances, our businesses, our churches, and other institutions. It has been exciting to *expand*. Now we must learn the difficult art of *contraction*.

Second—Concentrate on the *core* items of life: Health, Wealth, Relationships and Usefulness. These often interact. For example, a breakdown in relationships may cause a problem with our health. But we don't need unlimited amounts of any of these four items, only enough to be and do what God has planned for this season of our life.

Third—I then asked if there were any surprises, anything he hadn't expected when he entered this decade of life. He thought for a moment and then answered slowly, "Yes. It was much harder than I expected!"

As we concluded our talk, he did something that underscored why I had been drawn to call him for advice. This 80+ year old mentor wrote his telephone number on a piece of paper, handed it to my grandson and said, "Call me in 20 years and tell me how you're doing." Then he thought a moment and said, "Make that

10 years!" Surely, this is one of the wise, helpful, aged men that Moses and Plato had in mind.

During the intervening years, I have continued to talk with other older men and women. Some were reluctant, and some felt inadequate, but all have been helpful. I encourage you not to miss the resource of these older saints as you walk through life. As has been said, "There's no reason to spend your life reinventing the wheel."

What Specific Action Shall We Take to Prepare for Generation IV?

Here are some of the steps I took to be prepared to finish life's race. Perhaps they will help you consider the action you want to take in preparation for Generation IV.

1. Cutting and Pruning—John 15:2 says, "He cuts off every branch in me that bears no fruit, while every branch that does bear fruit he prunes so that it will be even more fruitful." I decided it was now time to cut and prune in my life. I agonized over each of the following decisions, and each stroke of the blade hurt. But I believe they were all necessary and will increase the fruit God will produce if I stay the course with him.

2. Occupation—I fully retired from the practice of law. Like Cortez who burned his ships on the beaches of Mexico, I filed my resignation with the courts so I wouldn't be tempted to set sail again.

3. Home—We moved into a new, smaller patio home designed for our older years.

4. Investments—We eliminated investments that required hands-on management.

5. Expenses—We cut about 30 percent from our preretirement budget.

6. Church—We moved into a new church experience that seemed to fit our new chapter of life.

7. Future Plans—Some time ago I heard a speaker graphically describe the loss of his wife and child. As he took us through the events and the months that followed, he concluded that we all need three things in life:

      a. Someone to love
      b. Something to do
      c. Something to look forward to

Younger men often ask, "Why are many older people so discouraged?" I am sure there are many reasons, including the physical, mental, and emotional infirmities that come with age. Those we often can't avoid. But we can address the three issues given by the speaker who was working through his great loss.

      a. Someone to love—I want to make every reasonable effort to keep close to my wife and family, my old friends, and to welcome new friends into my life.
      b. Something to do—I want to continue with the word-worker service God has entrusted to me, as

long as I am able, and with whomever he places around me.

c. Something to look forward to—I want to make plans for celebrations, events and activities as far in advance as possible. Like one 90-year old who bought a rug and demanded a fifteen year guarantee!

And I also want to look forward to Heaven when this life is over. May I be one in spirit with the Apostle Paul who said:

Forgetting what is behind and straining toward what is ahead,
I press on toward the goal to win the prize for which
God has called me heavenward in Christ Jesus.
(Philippians 3:13b, 14)

8. Final Arrangements—Making final arrangements for our property, personal possessions, and funeral, and choosing our burial site, are acts of kindness we shouldn't overlook. For thousands of years, burials and gravesites have been an integral part of the Bible and God's people. It is a final opportunity to show our care and respect for our loved ones and to establish a resting place to help connect our generations together. Acts 13:36 (emphasis added) says,

*For when David had served God's purpose **in his own generation**, he fell*
asleep; he was buried with his fathers and his body decayed.

I do not know when my generation will end, or what plans God has for me between now and that time. I would consider it a privilege to live to welcome the new millennium in the year 2000 A.D. (Note: I originally wrote this chapter shortly before the year 2000.) But I would consider it a greater privilege to go and be with Him.

One thing I *do* know is that God loves me, and He loves you. And He has a purpose for our lives as long as we live. Then—after we have served God's purpose—we, too, can fall asleep and go to be with Him, or He will come for us! What a hope! What a destination for eternity! And what a joy to be with Jesus and with our loved ones and all of you who have surrendered your lives to Him!

It's your turn, now, to look at these years from your perspective and consider what actions you believe are best for you and yours.

QUESTIONS

1. What plans do you need to make so you will "Be Ready" for the last part of your life—and eternity?

2. When and how will you complete those plans?

Generation IV:

A Time to Finish

Age 75–Onward

I have fought the good fight, I have finished the race, I have kept the faith.
Now there is in store for me the crown of righteousness,
which the Lord, the righteous Judge, will award to me on that day—
and not only to me, but also to all who have longed for his appearing.
(2 Timothy 4:7-8)

We come now to the late autumn of life. If God grants us these additional years, it is a time when many are allowed to move from being a grandparent to a great-grandparent. These are the days we can be "renewed" inwardly by growing closer to Jesus and others, even though outwardly we are "wasting away". (2 Corinthians 4:16). This is a time when we can continue to mature as we "run with perseverance the race marked out for us." (Hebrews 12:1)

ONWARD AND UPWARD
AGE 75–80

He gives strength to the weary and increases the power of the weak.
Even youths grow tired and weary, and young men stumble and fall;
but those who hope in the Lord will renew their strength.
They will soar on wings like eagles; they will run and not grow weary,
they will walk and not be faint.
(Isaiah 40:29-31)

A Stairway Up to Heaven
There's a stairway up to Heaven
It's the stairway of the Cross.
At first the steps seem hard
And sometimes you feel lost.
But as you climb on higher
Your strength begins to grow.
And then you soar above the earth
Where living waters flow.

My mother, who lived to age 85, once said, "I was worried that, when I got to be older, I wouldn't be able to do all the things that I wanted to do. But when I got to be older I found out that I didn't want to do them anyway!"

Our view of life at one season just doesn't seem to apply at a later season.

Out of the World
Just as I moved "Into the World" around age 25 I now found myself moving back "Out of the World" at age 75.

153

Since I was born in 1925, I reached age 75 and began Generation IV in the year 2000. We entered this new millennium with unbridled optimism following the end of the decades-long Cold War and financial markets climbing to all time high values during the 1990's. New Year's Eve, 1999, found the world basking in an unprecedented series of fireworks and massive celebrations as twelve o'clock midnight was celebrated around the globe via television, as each time zone reached the New Year. But the euphoria was short-lived. Within three years, the stock market bubble had burst; Islamic militants had successfully attacked the World Trade Center in New York and the Pentagon in Washington, DC; and our nation was at war against terrorism in Afghanistan and Iraq. In addition the cultural war over social values—particularly involving homosexuality and marriage—was sharply dividing our nation, as the United States Supreme Court outlawed state sodomy laws, and states began to approve same-sex marriage.

But age 75 found us largely out of the loop on these national and international issues. We had fought our wars in the previous decades. Many outside activities that were very significant to us, in their time, now seemed to have lost their luster. I discovered I had less desire to explore unknown places and meet new people and an increased desire to spend time with my family and old friends. When I asked one older man what he would have done differently during these later years, he thought a moment, and then he quietly responded, "I could have called my old friends for lunch more often."

We have renewed interest in reunions—whether for our families, High Schools and Colleges, military service, or longtime work places.

We send one another congratulations for golden anniversaries and lifetime achievement awards. We get new knees and new hip joints; we play less golf and tennis, and we take more pills and afternoon naps. We lose spouses, siblings, and lifelong friends. We read the obituary columns faithfully, and we write eulogies and letters of condolence. We often encounter acquaintances more at funerals than at social events. Our bodies grow weaker, our minds grow dimmer, and our ranks grow thinner. We hear the news media tell us that of the 16 million service men and women in World War II, only 4 million remain, and that we are dying at the rate of over 1000 per day. And we are painfully aware that we probably don't have too much time left!

(Note: As I reread this now in 2014 I discover there are less than two million veterans alive today. Before long we will **all** be history!)

Despite the sadness and sense of loss that sometimes surrounds us, I discovered that the beginning of this fourth quarter of life can also be an exhilarating time—much like the feeling I often had when I left earth to soar aloft in an airplane flight when I was still attached to this world's atmosphere, but now also detached from the earth itself, and able to see how much broader and more beautiful is this wonderful creation of God.

Turning toward Home

I found Age 75-80 to be a time when many of us decide to change direction and come closer to home. Some, who had moved away during earlier seasons of life, now return to spend their final years among familiar surroundings. Others, who had owned and enjoyed vacation homes, conclude it is time to sell or turn these over to the next generation.

Marriage, family, and friends now absorb much of the time, energy, and attention we previously poured out in the marketplace or into other outside institutions. Relationships were an area of life I thought would be good in these final years, but I had no way of knowing the inexpressible joy they were going to bring. I have concluded it is not something that can be accurately described. It must be experienced. I encourage you to work to make your relationships rich in your own final years.

As we entered retirement, you could hear some couples voicing concerns about too much togetherness. One wife's bumper sticker expressed her dilemma this way, "Retirement: Half as much money and twice as much husband!"

In order to solve the potential problem, many new retirees find refuge in volunteer work, golf, tennis or other diversionary activities away from the house. But by age 80, if we are fortunate enough to have each other, we are often much more concerned when we are *not* together. And you sometimes see older couples walking and talking together in the malls and parks, holding hands like newlyweds. By giving up our right to march to our own drumbeat, we have begun to experience a oneness that we could not fully comprehend in our earlier years. It is a sweet conclusion that is worth the wait.

Children, grandchildren and sometimes, great grandchildren (in both our physical and spiritual families) are now multiplying. We are increasingly aware that, when our last page is written, it will be our faith, and the way we interact with our wives and family that will be the greatest gift of love most of us can leave to the generations who follow.

And it is not only our physical family, but also our broader family, that becomes more and more important to us during this period. Bible Study groups, Couples Groups, Sunday Fellowships and rich friendships with individuals all deeply enhance our faith and our walk with the Lord. It becomes increasingly obvious that we cannot walk alone through life. I found it was important to let go of my ultra-independence, and embrace the marvelous community that is available if we give out of the strengths God has given to us, and be willing to receive from others what God has given them to share.

If we are spiritually aware, I believe these are the years when we not only desire to come home in this world, but also to come back home to God. As we gradually move away from the temporary things of the world, we find we have more opportunity to spend time with Him, and to complete the work for which we were created. And we also find ourselves quietly taking solace in the verses in Ecclesiastes that tell us God has made "everything" (which must include old folks) "beautiful" in their time.

As these five years from age 75 to 80 progressed, it seems as if the downward pull of earth's gravity is decreasing, and the upward pull of God's gravity is increasing, as He draws us toward Heaven and eternity with Him.

Ministering in the Last Part of Life

The concept of ministry by the laity is difficult at any stage of life, but it seems particularly elusive as we enter Generation IV. I hear some say they feel their ability to minister is gone. Others question whether they are needed any longer. And others are willing, but they don't know what God would have them do.

The term "minister" simply means to serve. Those who minister are servants. All followers of Jesus are to carry out this role. (See Philippians 2:5–7.) Although our abilities change as we age, and our thoughts gradually shift from earthly matters toward what lies ahead in Heaven, God will still use us here on earth if we are willing.

A few will probably be like Caleb who conquered the "hill country" at age 85 (See Joshua 14.)But most of us will find our strength declining and the need to minister in new and less physical ways. Here are a few areas that appear ripe for ministry in these later, less active, years. These are simple ways that we can continue to serve God and others without regard to our age, credentials, wealth, or ability to travel.

- Be a "Lover" The more we open our hearts, and accept God's love for us, the more we are able to love Him and others. (See 1 John.)
- Give "Thanks" The Bible seldom mentions *feeling* grateful, but *giving* thanks is a major theme. We bless others, as well as ourselves, when we openly express our thanks. (See 1 Thessalonians 5:18.)
- Be a Good "Model" When older people live and act in Godly ways, we can become models for those who follow us. (See Titus 2:2.)
- Be an "Encourager" Younger people are often searching for an older person to counsel them and to encourage them and to give them hope for the future. Sharing our lives and God's Word may change their lives for good. (See Psalm 71:18.)

- "Pray" The power and privilege of prayer are God's gift that doesn't cease until we go to be with Him. (See 1 Thessalonians 5:17.)
- Be a "Lasting Witness" Telling others what Jesus and His Spirit have done for us is a lifelong privilege. It seems more important to pass on our faith than our money. We may be God's messengers to future generations if we will preserve our testimony by writing or recording our journey. (See Acts 20:24.)

Finishing Well

Much has been discussed recently about finishing well. We all want that for our lives. But what is "well"? I don't think it means we have to finish physically strong, like Caleb. In fact many of us will be totally unable to function at the time we finish. The real issue is this, "Are we willing to finish our lives in the way God wants, regardless of our desires, or what others may say?"

Jesus understands that being His disciple is difficult, and that we will be tempted not to finish with Him. After discussing a man who was unable to finish a tower, and a king who was unable to finish a war, as recorded in Luke 14, Jesus concludes with these sobering words:

In the same way,
any of you who does not give up everything he has
cannot be my disciple.
(Luke 14:33)

I have concluded that finishing well does not require that we complete our lives and our work in a way that results in approval and recognition during our lifetimes—nor eulogies and monument markers that extol our accomplishments after we are gone. Instead I think our lives will be pleasing to God when we "give up everything" in this world and simply rely on Him and His grace to care for us, and to use us as He wishes. At first this sounds harsh and unrealistic, until we finally understand that He is drawing us onward and upward to a far better eternity with Him, when our short span of years here on earth is completed.

Conclusion

Thanks for taking this walk with me through these last five years. It has helped me immensely to put these events in focus. And I also thank the Lord, because I realize that my desire to *leave* the baggage of this world is becoming stronger than my desire to *keep* it! Perhaps that is one of God's gifts as we age. He causes our emphasis in life to change, and we want to soar aloft with Jesus more than we want to do the things of this world. As Mom said, "I found that I didn't want to do them anyway!"

I hope reading this has been helpful for you as you plan your own life journey. (And also as you work with older people who are walking through this time of life.) I do not know how you will decide to live the years of age 75-80. Your experience may be entirely different than mine. But I encourage you to consider the questions on the following page—not only for yourself but also for those ahead of you and for those who are following—so that when the time comes you will be prepared.

In the meantime, may God richly bless you as you continue your journey with Him. I look forward to seeing you in Heaven, if not before.

QUESTIONS

1. What does it mean to you to "Finish Well"?

2. What steps will you take to help that happen?

3. List the relationships that are most important to you right now. What can you do to invest in those relationships?

LETTING GO
AGE 80–85

In the same way,
any of you who does not give up everything he has
cannot be my disciple.
(Luke 14:33)

Consciously "letting go" really began for me when I surrendered my "will" and accepted Jesus forty years ago. It has never stopped! Since then He has called me to give Him control of many areas of life—including my wife, our children, the law practice, our money, personal rights, lifetime friends, and other items and activities once held dear. Now, as I reflect on the first five years of my 80's, I find the process of "letting go" has not only continued, but seems to have accelerated at an ever-increasing rate. And I expect it will continue until I am finally Home with Him.

During recent years I started to write about this subject, but it always seemed God wanted to show me more before I tried to pass it on. It was only after I had to "let go" of Ellie— my wife— this past year, that he finally seemed to say,

"It is OK. Since you have given up your lifetime love,
it is time for you to pass on what you have been learning."

What I am sharing is not meant to be all-inclusive, or a directive of what you should do, but merely some areas that stand out as I look back. My thoughts and words feel somewhat awkward and unfinished without Ellie's recollections and quiet counsel but, hopefully, the discussion will be helpful.

163

When I first surrendered to God in 1969, I had no idea what changes would be involved. Fortunately, they didn't occur all at once. Instead He graciously and lovingly unfolded the items to "let go", one by one, as we walked through the years together. Some have been relatively easy, others have been quite hard, but all have produced a life far above and beyond what I ever dreamed could happen.

So join me for a few minutes as we walk through several of these major areas where I faced "letting go" as an "act of the will." Some of these areas are deliberately repeated from earlier writings, but it seemed necessary to bring them together in this final chapter to comprehend the full and continuing impact this theme has had in my journey.

Wife

After "letting go" of myself, the most important challenge was to "let go" of Ellie. Although terribly difficult, it seemed timely and right to give her back to God last year. Her departure was "beautiful in its time" as promised in Ecclesiastes 3. But I have come to realize I also had to "let go" in a series of earlier, less dramatic, but very important ways.

I had always referred to her as "My Ellie"! Toward the end of her life, I finally realized she was "Our Ellie," because so many other people also loved her. But many years before that, I had my greatest learning experience when I comprehended she was first and foremost, "Her Own Ellie"! When I stopped trying, often unconsciously, to control her and began to depend on her to provide the other half of life I couldn't comprehend as a man, it helped our marriage flourish. God enriched us both as she counseled and I wrote *Complete—Don't Compete!" (The Biblical Roles of Husbands and Wives).*

(Note: This is available on my website *"fromgrandpawithlove.com"* and will be a part of the book on *Marriage* mentioned in the Personal Note at the beginning of this book.)

It came at a heavy price and with many tears but—amid the tears— she made two statements that cemented the need to release and respect her as her own person: "Don't you understand? I'm a woman!" And, "Don't you understand? I'm a reactor!" I never forgot either, and it changed our lives and those around us.

Through all the years of loving and living, one fundamental lesson kept emerging:

> *The more I "let go" of Ellie,*
> *the more she loved me and tried to help me,*
> *because she wanted to be with me,*
> *and not because I was trying to control her.*

And now that she is gone, I am confident God will supply all my needs until we are joined again in Heaven.

Children

I have concluded it is difficult—No! It is impossible, at least for me—to raise children with just the right amount of control and help, and then "let go" and gradually release them so they can be and do what God has planned for their lives. Looking back, I know now that it only began to *really* work for me when I "let go" and trusted God to guide, direct and bring them through life. I have never tried to write anything about raising children. We strive and do all we can, but looking back, I am convinced it really happens by the grace of God. But Ellie and I rejoiced and thanked Him, our children and everyone who poured into their lives when we saw the results. Sometimes I think it is like shooting fireworks into the sky, and then watching in wonder at all the power and beauty that blazes forth high above us—and knowing it is now all totally out of our control!

It has taken many years, lots of trial and error, and some frank conversations with some of our children for me to see how subtly I can try to keep controlling them long after I should have "let go". Here are a few examples that remind me I will probably need to work at releasing our children as long as I live. Maybe they will help you.

- Early on I gave a gift of physical tools to one child rather than something I would have preferred to own. The response was sincere and heartfelt, "Thank you for giving me what *I* wanted instead of what *you* preferred!"

- Later as I concluded a call in which I voiced some concern over a proposed course of action by one of our "just-grown" children, I ended by saying, "Thanks for the call." The quiet response was, "*I* didn't call you, Dad. *You* called me!"

- Recently I discussed the earlier years with one of our children and said (probably a little self-righteously), "I don't think I ever tried to control what you should decide when you were to make decisions." The response was a classic, "No, you never *told* me what to decide. But you made me *feel* stupid if I didn't do it!"

As our children matured, I learned much of my contribution to their well-being was to love, pray, give perspective, and listen. I also decided that "raising" grandchildren and great grandchildren is usually not my business. It may make me look and feel "greater," but it may cause the parent to look and feel "lesser." My good intentions may actually usurp and tend to nullify the parents' own sense of purpose and the chance to carry out a major part of their own life work. After our children left home, I concluded my job was mostly to "let go" and to "love" them and their families. Again the same general principle was proving to be true with our children as it had been for my own life and for my relationship with Ellie.

The more I "let go" of our children as they matured,
the more I sensed our love and friendship grow.

Law Practice

The Law Practice was another major area where I had to "let go." It basically happened in two stages. I have written about the first decision that took place about age 50, when I decided to take an open stand for Christ. The second stage occurred at about age 60, as I "let go" and began to phase out and move fully into retirement.

After taking the four major steps described in the "Harvest Time" chapter—no more trial work, no more firm management, no more acquisition of capital, and setting a time table to sell my interest in the firm at Age 65 and retire at Age 70 —the results were similar to those in the other areas.

When I "let go" of the law practice, it allowed others in the firm to grow and gave me the opportunity to concentrate my older years on eternal issues.

Money

Money was always a tool for me rather than a goal. But we do need it to live and function, so I spent many years trying to make what we needed and put some aside for our later years. As I mentioned, I have concluded it is often not people who *spend* money who love it. Instead, it seems more likely it is the people who *don't want to part with it.* The harsh realization for me was that I loved money when I didn't want to "let go" of it.

I was taught to be self reliant, and I expected others to do the same. Taking care of our own family was a given, but giving to others was a somewhat foreign concept to me. Gradually I realized,—by watching the generosity of others and by Bible truths, such as the stories in Luke 12 and 18 about two rich men who didn't want to "let go" of their wealth—that I needed to give to others in need. And there were times to give generously and profusely to do something "beautiful" for God—like the woman in Mark 14 who poured perfume on Jesus that was worth a year's wages. And I found it all worked best when I "let go" of others responsibilities and allowed everyone to spend and give as they were led—not as I thought best!

In addition I concluded, somewhat reluctantly, that we should gradually invade our principal (i.e., the money we had invested) to provide for our later years. This was against all I thought had been right. But the need to obey God's directives about "scattering" in Genesis 11, Ecclesiastes 3, and Acts 8 overruled my objections.

So, I set an imaginary life span of 100 years, and calculated what should be spent and given each year, based on investment income (hopefully 5 percent), plus deliberately eroding the principal except for a reasonable margin to remain at the end. Who knows—we might live to 105! But also keeping in mind one financial collapse, one war, one electronic blip and all our investments could be wiped out, anyway!

It was amazing what peace of mind God's direction gave when the stock market crashed recently. Again, the adage of "letting go" was proving true as it became clear:

The more I "let go" and trusted God to provide through safe, prudent investments, the less I was subject to market fluctuations and the more freedom I had to love, live, speak and write for Him and others!"

I did decide on three rather basic times I believe it helps to "let go" of "our" money, if we want God to use it the most—not necessarily by us but rather through all those whom He allows us to reach during our time here on earth:

1. "Letting go" *before* we make it, so we can help others also make some.
2. "Letting go" *while* we make it, so the stream stays fresh.
3. "Letting go" *after* we have stored it up, so it all gets "scattered" by the end.

Personal Rights

As I aged it seemed that everywhere I turned it was time to "let go" of other areas of life, and often they were personal rights to which I was clinging. Life became much easier, after I began to "let go" of what I expected to receive from others, and began to concentrate on what I was to do for them, following Jesus' example in Philippians 2, in areas such as:

Love—"Let go" of the right to be loved, but still love others.

Thanks—"Let go" of the right to be thanked, but still thank others.

Serving—"Let go" of the right to be served, but still serve others.

Forgiveness—"Let go" of the right to be forgiven, but still forgive others.

Mercy—"Let go" of the right to expect mercy, but still show mercy to others.

Honor—"Let go" of the right to be honored, but still honor others.

Comfort—"Let go" of the right to be comforted, but still comfort others.

Somehow, it has become more natural to release all of these during the last five years, as the World has receded and Heaven has drawn nearer. Again, the principle of "letting go" of the Kingdom of the World, has blessed me and those around me as I discovered:

The more I "let go" of my "personal rights" and concentrated on others, the more I received the contentment and peace which God has promised.

Friends

I expected the immense sorrow and loss I would experience when it came time to "let go" of Ellie. But I never quite realized the sorrow that would come from the steady drumbeat of "letting go" of lifetime friends—especially the rush of leaving which has occurred during these last five years. I have one group of twenty friends who began meeting about fifty years ago, and we have lost ten of those friends—three of them during this last year. The statement in Psalm 90 that our years are "…eighty, if we have the strength…" is proving true indeed. And I miss each friend who leaves!

But if we really believe that Heaven is better than this World, and that going Home to be with Jesus and all the saints is the destination we have been moving toward all our lives, surely it can only be sorrow for ourselves, not for those who have left for Home. And so another blessing appeared in the midst of our loss.

The more I "let go" of our friends, the more I can rejoice for them when they reach the shores of Heaven and all it holds— and the more I cherish those who still remain with us!

How good it will be to greet the saints when we join them all for eternity.

A Smaller Circle

As we discussed earlier, an older friend told me I would need to manage "deterioration" as we aged. It was good advice. By the time I reached age 80, my abilities and my circle of loved ones had shrunk. And the process has accelerated even more during these last five years. But each narrowing experience also had its blessing. Here are some examples.

- <u>Home</u>—Shortly after I reached age 80, Ellie calmly announced, "It is time to go to Larksfield" (a senior center)—and we did. Our children helped us immeasurably, but leaving our home and most of our possessions and moving to a much smaller apartment was like a death. But it was a good trade. When we "let go," it freed us to enjoy these last few years with fewer cares about home ownership, safety, weather, etc; it gave us a community close at hand when going out became more difficult; and it provided us with emergency help if it became necessary.
- <u>Writings.</u> After some soul searching about motives, I removed my name from booklet covers, and placed the writings God gave me on a free website, "www.fromgrand-pawithlove.com." By "letting go" of the materials He has *given,* they were able to blow free wherever the wind takes them. And I was able to be with Ellie and do some extra writing, at the same time other activities declined.
- <u>Organizations</u>. Clubs and organizations provide relationships and sometimes an illusion of status. A series of resignations allowed us to "let go" of community activities, and concentrate on the smaller world we had entered. Simply being together became far more important than what we were doing during each day.
- <u>Travel.</u> When we were younger, travel was exciting. As we aged, it became a burden. As we "let go" of "going", we had more time for God and people. As we saw our time drifting away, it was no contest.

- Health and Mobility. Age takes its toll on our mental and physical abilities. Everyone is different, but the key to contentment for us seemed to depend largely on whether we embraced each chapter or fought it. When Ellie and I accepted her "long goodbye", and "let go" of what we could no longer do, it became one of the great periods of our life. A time for loving, with nothing much to interfere.
- Interdependence. God calls us to "interdependence", more than "independence" or "dependence". We each need only to be able to do what God is calling us to do at that stage of life. "Letting go" and relying on others as needed during these past few years, has been another unexpected blessing.

What Happens Next?

As I sat by Ellie's bedside during her final days last September, I thought of many things. One, of course, was about dying. As I reminisced about our lives together, I began to think of those who had gone before us. I mused to myself, "All Ellie's family and ancestors have died. Ellie is going to die. All my folks and ancestors are gone, and I am going to die." Then I added thoughtfully, "Since everybody is going to die, we had better get this figured out!!"

The conclusion I have reached for myself is rather simple, yet satisfying:
Death is a fact of life; it is totally natural; I am to accept it, try and prepare for it,
and hope to be at peace with God and others all the time,
so whenever it is time finally to "let go", I am ready.

Shortly after I prayed and surrendered my will to God at age 44, I prayed a companion prayer which was really a desperate plea:

"Now that you've found me, Lord, don't let me go!"

What I didn't realize at that time was that the two prayers go hand in hand:

I only allow God to care for me to the extent that
I "let go" of my will and take hold of His hands!

I once heard it compared to a trapeze act. As we swing through the air, we "let go" of one bar and turn around and take hold of the strong outstretched hands waiting to carry us safely to the other side. But we have to "let go" first!

After Ellie left last year, I felt rudderless. I knew I had been privileged to be with her until she reached the other shore. But, then it was as if Jesus took the boat and put me back out on the river. When I asked for direction, I seemed to get the same simple answer He so often offers those who are searching:

"You must follow me."
(John 21:22b)

So that is what I intend to do.

One old jokester friend of mine commented recently, "At our age it is pretty hard to sin much anymore." Not true! But I know what he meant. Since I am getting close to the end and have let go of many of life's substitutes, the issue is increasingly how to hold on until God calls me Home. I have decided, therefore, not only to continue "letting go" of the world but also to concentrate even more on holding on to God's hands. Here again I am thankful for one of Ellie's favorite scriptures that I hope to apply, until God calls me and I "let go" one last time!

So take a new grip with your tired hands, stand firm on your shaky legs, and mark out a straight, smooth path for your feet so that those who follow you, though weak and lame, will not fall and hurt themselves, but become strong.
(Hebrews 12:12, Living Bible)

Now, it is time to answer the following questions which are designed to aid you in applying our discussion to your lives. I pray they help.

QUESTIONS

1. What are the areas of life where you have already "Let Go"?

2. What areas of life are you still holding, which you would like to "Let Go"?

3. What actions should you take to "Let Go" of these remaining areas?

A CLOSING THANK YOU

It has now been over three years since I reached Age 85 and completed the journey you just traveled with me. For some time I have known I needed to place all this in a permanent record for my family and others who may be interested. At first I thought I might wait and add another five year chapter from Age 85-90, or perhaps even be optimistic and finalize it at Age 95. But then reality set in.

During the last few years I have increasingly felt the chill winds of winter coming on, and I concluded God was telling me to get it done while I am still well enough to do so. In addition, our thinning ranks make it clear the odds of most readers reaching Age 90 or beyond are pretty slim and any extra chapters would not help very many folks.

Perhaps most importantly, Age 85 seems a natural break point coming shortly after the death of my dear wife, Ellie, who shared 61 years of marriage, family and most of my lifetime experiences. While God has graciously given me some additional time and a good remarriage, these additional years seem more of a postscript than a continuation of life as we have known it. We are still connected to our loved ones here. But it is almost as if they were helping us prepare for the ultimate adventure as we move into our space ship with a final crew and get ready to head for Home. There may be a time He wants me to write about this later phase of life, but for now it is time to stop my story.

I hope you have enjoyed our journey together. The real purpose of the account is not that you will know my experiences (although it is good for us all to be aware of our family history); instead, the real benefit will come if it helps you look ahead and make decisions about your life from a positive and eternal perspective.

I lay it down with a profound sense of gratitude to God and to the family, friends and others who have been so gracious and generous to me throughout my life. You have all given me much more than I ever expected or deserved. For years my question to God has been, "Why me, Lord?"—not in the sense of being deprived, but rather being so undeservedly blessed!

It is, of course, sobering to see childhood, adulthood, maturity and old age all wrapped up in a few pages. It has caused me to ask again, "What was the purpose—and has it made any difference that I was here?" For me the answer is a resounding, "Yes!" Not in the sense of worldly accomplishments, but rather from all the relationships God has allowed me to have with Him and all the dear people He has placed in my life over the years..

I am content as I near the end. I am aware the consequences of both the good and bad I have done will affect those who are around and following me. I grieve for the wrong, but I know God has forgiven me. I have also come to realize the good and bad of preceding generations are personal blessings and curses each of us must work through as we travel across life's stage. So I am at peace.

Whatever additional time He grants me, I pray I will continue the simple but profound assignment He gave me on May 7, 1990—*to love people and to love God*! If that happens, it will bring glory to

Him, help others and complete the reason He placed me here on this earth for these eight decades.

See You in Heaven!

Marvin J. Martin
Wichita Kansas
2014

FOUR GENERATIONS

"Life Line"
Ezra 7:10

Generation I
"Learn"

Generation II
"Do"

Generation III
"Teach"

Generation IV
"Finish"

0 5 10 15 20 25 30 35 40 45 50 55 60 65 70 75 80 85 90 95

APPENDIX

A World War II Diary

Reliving "B-29" Memories
June 1945–June 1946

There is a time for everything...
a time for war and a time for peace.
(Ecclesiastes 3:1, 8)

CONTENTS

A PERSONAL NOTE

I recently reviewed an old World War II Diary I kept sporadically during my overseas service over 60 years ago. The record begins June 24, 1945, at our B-29 Base at Grand Island, Nebraska preparing to leave for Guam, and ends with my return "State side" on June 16, 1946, and "separation" from service on June 19, 1946. Since those of us who served in World War II are fast disappearing, it seemed appropriate to pass on some of the Diary to those who follow.

To keep the account as interesting as possible, only the entries which seemed most meaningful are included. Except for a few corrections, the excerpts are as written in the Diary. Explanatory comments are written in italics and placed throughout the account. A Glossary is included to help explain some of the terms.

The story must begin with my heartfelt gratitude to my father J.C. Martin (1877-1951) and my mother Bertha L. Martin (1894-1979). Their three sons (Leon, Claude and I) all joined the Army Air Corps, later known as the Air Force, during World War II. Mom kept a "Mother's Flag" with three stars on it, in the window. When Leon was killed in a B-24 air crash over England in March, 1945, the middle star became "gold". A few weeks later she and Dad uncomplainingly watched me head overseas. Their unfailing love, faith and fortitude modeled for me much of what it means to be a parent. Their actions deeply impacted the rest of my life.

Please accept what is recorded in the following pages as a personal letter and gift from my generation to yours.

Marvin J. Martin
Wichita, Kansas
2008

DEDICATION

This account is dedicated to the memory of all those who were injured or who lost their lives or loved ones during World War II. We owe you more than words can ever express.

Greater love has no one than this,
that he lay down his life for his friends.
(John 15:13)

THE B-29 CREW

Front Section of Aircraft
Aircraft Commander—Pilot in command of the B-29
Pilot—Second Pilot
Navigator—Tracked location and charted flight course
Bombardier—Operated visual Norden Bomb Sight
Radar Observer—Operated Radar to Bomb/Navigate
Flight Engineer—Maintained engines/fuel consumption
Radioman—Radio communications

Rear Section of Aircraft
Right Scanner—Visual check of engines/other aircraft
Left Scanner—Visual check of engines/other aircraft
Tailgunner—Operated tail gun.

GLOSSARY

Very General Descriptions of Some Terms

(Some Definitions Also Appear in the Diary Account)

Abort	Inability to start/complete scheduled missions
BOQ	Bachelor Officers' Quarters
Buzz	Fly toward some object with loud engines
Calibration	Adjusting instruments for accuracy
Chappie	Chaplain
DNIF	"Do not fly" status
Ditch	Crash land an airplane in the ocean
Drift	Amount wind blows plane off its heading
E.M.	Enlisted men
Empire	Japanese Homeland
Final	Last approach as a plane prepares to land
Fix	Determining a plane's location on a map
Flak	Anti-aircraft shells exploding at altitude
Flak curtain	Material used to protect against shell bursts
Flak suit	Clothing used to protect against shell bursts
G.I	Government Issue
G.I. ed	Washing the floor with a bristle G.I. brush
G.S.	Ground speed
Hubba-Hubba	WWII Exclamation used for emphasis!
IP	Initial Point of Bomb Run
Landfall (LF)	Point where plane enters the coastline
LCI	"Landing Craft Infantry" Naval vessel
Loran	Long range navigational aid

Mess Hall	Area where we ate our meals
Mickey	AN/APQ-7 radar and its operator.
MP	Military Police
#1,#2,#3,#4	Identification numbers for B-29 engines
Pre-Fabs	Barracks we assembled to house personnel
Points	System to determine priority to go home
P.P.	A cliché for "really bad"
Rate check	Preparation for releasing bombs accurately
RON	Remain Over Night
Rope	Streamers to deflect search lights and guns
Sack	Bunk where we slept
Wind run	Checking drift to release bombs accurately
Scope	Visible face of radar set.
Short Snorter	Money from many places pasted together
Socked In	Weather too bad to allow landing.
Time	24 hour clock without a.m. or p.m.
T.G.	Bombing Target
10 in1 Rations	Pre packaged food supplies
T.S.	A cliché for "tough luck"
Tunnel	Cylindrical crawl space above bomb bays

INTRODUCTION

Heading overseas was the culmination of over 2 years preparation. During World War II, we were allowed to enlist at age 17½ and choose our branch of service, to be called up for duty when we reached age 18. I chose the Army Air Corps and enlisted with a group of friends in February, 1943. Several of us left for active duty in September, 1943.

We took several weeks of Basic Training at Biloxi, Mississippi; extra schooling and dual flight training at Lansing Michigan; and additional testing at San Antonio, Texas to determine which classification (Pilot, Navigator or Bombardier) we would study. I was assigned to Navigation training at San Marcos, Texas, where I received my wings and commission as a 2nd Lt in November, 1944. I had additional Radar training at Boca Raton, Florida, followed by a shortened Bombardier Training course at Victorville, California. Finally, by June, 1945, I was ready to join a B-29 combat crew as a Radar Observer, and head for the Pacific.

I was assigned to the 411th Bomb Squadron (15 B-29's) of the 502nd Bomb Group (45 B-29's) which was part of the 315th Bomb Wing of the 20th Air Force to be located on the newly constructed Northwest Airfield on the island of Guam. The B-29's had been designed and built, many of them in our home town of Wichita, Kansas, for long range bombing missions against the Japanese homeland, since it was out of range for the smaller B-17 and B-24 four engine Bombers used so extensively in Europe and other areas.

The 502nd Group had been in operation and training for many months before I arrived at our gathering point in Grand Island,

Nebraska. Crews were assembled there and final preparations were made to receive our aircraft and leave for Guam.

I was 19 years old when we left the "States" and 20 years old when I returned. My "combat service" was brief: 2 "Island missions" and 3 "Empire missions" against the Japanese homeland (including the last and longest mission of WWII), all of which took place in the closing weeks of the War. In the months that followed we had the opportunity to make other peacetime flights to the Philippines, Okinawa, Hokkaido Japan, Iwo Jima and other Pacific bases. Our group lost only one plane in combat over Japan, but others were lost in accidents or at sea.

As I look back now, at age 82, on those long ago days, it is with a great sense of gratitude for what I received during those few years in the service. I am also glad that I recorded and saved my old Diary which has refreshed and brought back so many memories. Hopefully, it will also be of some interest and benefit to you who are reading this account.

So, I invite you now to come and relive with me some of the experiences that I recorded so many years ago as part of the youthful "Adventure" that helped give me my manhood during my Age 18-21 year chapter of life.

I trust the account is interesting enough to keep your attention—but as I once heard a speaker say, "I came to talk, you came to listen. If you finish before I do, feel free to leave!"

Hubba Hubba

Chapter 1

A New B-29
June 24–July 2, 1945

Sunday, June 24, 1945

Well, today started the long trek half-way cross the world—From Grand Island Neb. to "Destination Unknown"—somewhere in the S.W. Pacific.

We left GIAAF *(Grand Island Army Air Field)* at 1000 *(10:00 a.m.)* and arrived at Kearney *(Nebraska)*—after giving the tower the traditional Buzz Job—in TRUCKS—Yes—we left in trucks! Ha Ha. Some joke.

Arriving at Kearney we discovered that 3 of the 402nd Bomb Squadron were still here. They left Grand Island 3 weeks ago and had 6 "Fly-Aways" *(Planes which had left)*. We have 3 ships *(We often referred to our planes as "ships")* awaiting us & only 10 crews so our last ship won't probably get away for at least 2 weeks. (We are 6th priority) *(We flew out in the order of our priority number)*.

Monday, June 25, 1945

We really had fun processing today. I have 2 B-4 Bags full—Really full and I can only take one—trouble- trouble. Ha Ha—We got some really swell equipment. New B-4's, *(bags for clothing and personal articles)* A-3's *(Parachute bags)* & complete new flying outfit. Looks like we might be headed for combat. Ha Ha

Thursday, June 28, 1945

Found out we got the ship today. Really hope it is a good one. It should be—#4483915. Some of the fellows are getting the old #600 series & we end up with a #900—Pretty sharp, Huh?

> _Note:_ The B-29 was the "top of the line" both in size and comfort. It was an enlarged version of the earlier B-17 "Flying Fortress" built by Boeing. It was sometimes called the "Super Fortress". Standing next to it made you feel rather small—and you wondered if anything that size could fly: 99 feet long, over 29 feet high, (as tall as a two story house) with a wing span of 141 feet and weighing over 100,000 pounds. With pressurized cabins it could bomb from 30,000'. It cruised at over 200 mph, depending upon altitude. I don't remember why the "900" model was more advanced, but I know we were happy to have it.

Friday, June 29, 1945

We flew the "Big Iron Bird" today for the first time. Typical:

Got up 0500. Briefed at 0600. Went to ship and started to preflight—only to find that #2 turbo was surging (_malfunctioning_). Soooo—at 1400 we finally got off only to land at 1430 with fuel pressure on #3 and 4 way too high. Stood by until 1700 and then came back to the BOQ. We brief again in the morning at 0700.

> _Note:_ Most of the losses in our B-29 Group related to weather, mechanical, and engine problems. I suppose that was unavoidable in wartime when planes and flying crews were produced in mass quantities.

The Captain who briefed us this morning was some character. He practically told us that if we didn't like the way he ran the show we could go straight to _____. We stuck around.

Saturday, June 30, 1945

We flew again today and had much better luck. We had a fine calibration on the instruments (*adjusting for accuracy*) and my "Mickey" (*AN/APQ-7 radar set*)) was working fine. It is off a little but am having it fixed before we leave.

> *Note: We were using new secret radar equipment (referred to as the AN/APQ-7) that had been developed for precision bombing at night and through overcast conditions. The radar aerial was located in an eighteen-foot "wing" under the plane. It utilized a technique called "synchronous radar bombing." I sat in the front section of the aircraft—next to the navigator and behind the pilots—where I could view a pie-shaped scope, which showed bodies of water, land, and congregations of buildings that were in front of us. The target information from this equipment was then fed to the pilots and to the bombardier and his Norden bombsight in the nose of the plane. At the appropriate time, the bombs would be released from the bomb bays in the center of the aircraft. By today's standards it would be primitive; in 1945 it was "state of the art"!*

> *The equipment was also used as a navigation aid—particularly in finding the plane's position wherever land and water met. In addition it was helpful in turbulent weather since the heavy rain clouds would show up on the scope, and the radar could be used to help navigate around and through the thunder clouds— especially at night.*

<u>Monday, July 2, 1945</u>

"Skip to my Lou"—Tomorrow is the Big Day. We loaded today and leave for APOE (*airport where we will embark for overseas*) tomorrow—then xxxxxxxxxxxxxxxxxxxx (*scratched out the destination for security reasons*). Not much of a rumor anymore that the destination is xxxxxxxxx because they even let them write it on letters coming from there.

Everyone is sorry yet anxious to be going. Can't help but have just a tinge of sadness mixed in when you realize that some of your buddies won't make it back.

> <u>Note:</u> *I guess it never dawned on me that it might be me who wouldn't make it!*

I hope that someday in some way we will really have peace. All we can do now is fly the course that has been charted.

Chapter 2

From Nebraska to Guam
July 3–July 16, 1945

Tuesday, July 3, 1945 **Mather Field**
Got up at 0430. Cleaned up and ate. Caught the bus at 0530. I thought it was to be there at 0600 so I was the last man on.

Took off (*from Kearney*) around 0730 and arrived here (*Mather Field, California*) at 1030. (*Actually 5 hour trip because of change in time.*) Gave Kearney a big buzz job on the way. This time on a B-two-nine—(Better than a truck, anyway. Ha Ha)

Wednesday, July 4, 1945
No fireworks nor "nuttin". Just can't understand—However, I hear there are lots of fireworks where we are going. I understand they are mad at each other out there. Just so they don't scratch up our airplane—because—if they do we are going to be awfully bitter.

> *Note;* *I don't know if I was a very cocky young man or just trying to "whistle in the dark" because I was so frightened. Probably a little of both.*

We will leave probably tomorrow nite. We don't know yet. If we don't we will get passes (*to visit the town*) from 1600 to 0230. Just like being a "Kaydet" (*Air Corps Cadet*) again.

Hope we get started soon as that will make it that much sooner we go home.

Friday, July 6, 1945

We expected to leave tonite—But – Had a bad fuel pump—in fact two—They have to send to Oak City to get them!

SOoooo—I guess we will be here awhile. Vacation!

I guarded the airplane tonite. Some sack. I tried to sleep with the pilot's back cushions under me—They are rounded so I literally "rolled and tossed" Ha Ha—The tunnel doesn't work if one sleeps on one's stomach because one's arms aren't double jointed and one is liable to fracture one, isn't one—Huh? Wasn't so bad, tho—I finally just slept on the floor—Nothing to it.

> *Note:* We apparently were responsible for our plane's ground security as we headed overseas.

Saturday, July 7, 1945

We washed the airplane and she really shines. I noticed several ships back from their missions. Flying sometimes every day. That would be rough—getting home in 4-6 months would offset it. I don't care if it is 14 (*months*) tho, if we all get back O.K..

Wednesday, July 11, 1945

I think today is the day. We are scheduled to leave the good old U.S.A. tonite. Hope we get gone as it will be that much sooner that we get back. We signed out in the "Big Brown Book" at the Canteen. (*Probably unofficial*) We decided to call the ship "the Big Hutch" of the "Ten Wittle Wabbits"

> *Note:* Old pictures reveal other ships with names such as "The Uninvited" and "Just One Mo Time". Our name doesn't sound

very "military"—in fact I never thought it was a very exciting choice. But at the time it must have sounded right to us as our "home" in the air.

When Bob finished writing it in he put at the bottom, "Left these United States 11, July 1945—Returned—Damn Soon!"

Hope he is right!!!

Thursday, July 12, 1945

Well—Third times a charm. We finally got off—at 0530 after two tries. First thing—that fuel pump went bad.

Note: As you read on through the pages of the Diary, you can understand more and more why we lost airplanes due to mechanical difficulties in the months ahead.

We arrived in the "Beautiful and romantic islands of Hawaii" (end of commercial.) this afternoon. We were too early for regular mess but they fed us anyway. Not bad food at all. It was much better than I had expected. Only 40 cents too. We eat out of trays but the E.M.s have to use their mess gear. Too bad. I don't like all this distinction.

We get off tomorrow so we will go to "Lulu" (*Honolulu*).

Friday, July 13, 1945

Friday the 13th—maybe it is supposed to be unlucky—Not for me, tho—For today I saw—Waikiki—(With 10,000,000,000 others- Ha Ha)

Actually, tho, we had a very pleasant day. Started for Hickam Field (*a Japanese target on December 7, 1941*) about noon. (Bev, Jules & I). We ate lunch at Hickam (which was very nice) and then went on to "Lulu". Bus service is poor. But an M.P. stopped a G.I. truck for us. Honolulu itself is P.P. so we went on out to Waikiki. That is really a nice spot. I imagine before the war it was a paradise. I took a whole roll of film. Sure hope it turns out O.K.

> *<u>Note:</u> Some of our family visited Honolulu in the 1980's. We asked the cab driver to take us by the Royal Hawaiian Hotel, which I recalled as being set off by itself and the "swanky" hotel in 1945. He smiled and drove us by the hotel I remembered, but it was now dwarfed by huge multi story buildings surrounding it. How times change!*

Saturday, July 14, 1945
We were to leave Honolulu N.A.S at 0830. We were awakened at 0430, ate, "briefed" and went to take off. Same old thing–? ——

———————————

"Nope"—Fooled you! The flap motor burned up. We finally got off about 1100. Really a long stretch of "Nothing". Only one island in about 2000 miles. It was about 1/3 of the way there. We really hit everything on the nose tho.

Sunday, July 15, 1945
We lost a day along in here. We took off in the morning— landed in the afternoon of the same day—But it is SUNDAY. Going back we will probably "leave tomorrow and arrive yesterday."

Note: In later years, Ellie and I could never understand why she thought the War ended on August 14, and I was sure it was August 15. It finally dawned on us that we were both right—we had just been on opposite sides of the International Date Line! It was a good example of something I now realize happens too often, particularly in Bible discussion. Folks fight about which statements are true when each is stating a "truth" but not the "whole truth".

This is about the sorriest place I have ever seen. I am now speaking of the beautiful little island (or atoll) Ha of Kwajalein. I would sure hate to be stationed there.

If you think barn yards stink, you should have smelled their latrines—Whew__

They had a sharp Officer's Club. The porch was practically on the ocean. (The Island was so thin I think the back steps went in to the water, too)

Monday, July 16, 1945
Got up at 0600. Ate, briefed, took off around 0930. We thought we were pretty sharp when we finally reached destination (Guam), with no trouble & hit every island on the nose. Over 6000 miles with NO TROUBLE.

Arrived at Harmon Field (*on Guam*) about 1400 their time. Ate lunch, unloaded the mail and prepared to take off for a long trip—6 miles up to N.W (*Northwest*) field.

Before taking off we talked to a little Guamanian boy. He had worked for the Japs (*a common term for "Japanese" during WWII*) when they were here. They killed his little bro. and were preparing to kill him when he escaped & hid in the hills.

Note: When we landed at Northwest Field, we found a rather new area recently carved out of the jungle. At the beginning, we lived in tents, and since there were hundreds of men and no women we had outdoor showers, consisting of long overhead pipes with occasional shower heads and cold water. We also had outdoor latrines. The urinals were pipes stuck into the ground with funnels at the top. The "stools" we used were in small huts, marked "Officers Latrine". Enlisted men had their own facilities. There were also some metal Quonset buildings. After the war ended the area was upgraded with prefabricated buildings. There were also some metal Quonset buildings.

Chapter 3

Two Island Air Raids
July 17–27, 1945

Tuesday July 17, 1945
Didn't have much to do today. Built a floor for the tent and took all my stuff out of my B-4 Bag. Went over and got my footlocker (*Sent earlier by boat*) and unpacked it. Everything was still in it.

Rained a couple of times. It does every day I guess. Just lasts about 5 minutes at a time. Then blows over and sun shines. One of these days it will be coming down in torrents.

> *Note: During the months we were on Guam, it did rain a lot. Until the war ended they showed movies out of doors. When the heavy rains began, we simply pulled our ponchos over our heads and kept right on watching the show.*

They say there are still a lot of Japs on the Island. The Marines are chasing them from one end to the other.

Wednesday, July 18, 1945
Today we found out we would bomb entirely radar sync. Even if the TG (*target*) "breaks" (*becomes visible*) we will still drop by "Mickey". With only water, pilotage is "practically" "impossible".

> *Note: The new Radar had the obvious benefit of being able to "see" when darkness or clouds prevented seeing through the Norden Bombsight. I don't know if those in charge were trying*

to test the new radar synchronization system for accuracy, or perhaps they felt the combination of Radar and the Norden was better than simply using the older visual method.

Caught and had to censor mail today. Everyone is lonesome!

Note: During WWII it was common to censor mail to blank out any sensitive information. Flying Officers were sometimes selected for this extra duty. I obviously wasn't pleased to have been chosen. I must have been at the wrong place at the wrong time, so I got caught and had to read a batch of outgoing letters. Apparently being lonesome was a common theme of many of the letters.

Thursday, July 19, 1945
No mail yet. I'm not discouraged, tho. Some of the boys were here 2 wks before any arrived.

They are really pushing us. We were scheduled for the "ditching" (*crash landing the plane at sea*) practice drill but didn't know it – so – we haven't been yet. They are letting us go ahead and fly our training missions until we can get a chance to make it up.

The boys seem to be having very little trouble on their "Empire Missions"—Haven't lost any planes due to enemy action. Lost several due to engine trouble and fire.

Note: Our runways ended at the edge of a several hundred foot cliff going down to the ocean. It gave us extra time to get up air speed after takeoff, but it also could cause us to crash

and burn if we didn't get airborne by the end of the runway,
because there was no margin to slow down and come to a stop.

Friday, July 20, 1945

Charlie went on his Truk (*Island*) mission tonite. Got back
about 0600 Saturday morn. Said he had no trouble at all—
except they couldn't find the I.P. I pray to God that none of
the missions cause more trouble.

We fly our first mission tomorrow. Just a practice mission. We
are bombing Pagan Island. Seems to be a good target.

We drop 6 single release radar sync (*using the radar set*) and 5
visual (*using the Norden Bomb Sight*). Most have had good luck.
Hope we do! They are 250 lb G.P.s (*I think this meant "General*
Purpose") so we should be able to see them.

> *Note: The entry seems callous and uncaring about the people*
> *being bombed, but because we bombed from a high altitude we*
> *never had a sense of what we were destroying down below—*
> *only a desire to hit the target as we had been trained to do.*
> *In later years I thought about the number of people who had*
> *been involved, directly and indirectly, when we released our*
> *bombs: those who built and maintained the planes, bombs and*
> *equipment; trained, fed and outfitted the crews; built the airfields*
> *and delivered the gasoline and supplies; grew the crops and meat*
> *we ate, and made the clothes we wore. The list was endless. It*
> *made me realize I didn't accomplish anything on my own—and*
> *I didn't drop the bombs on my own. It didn't make our "bombs*
> *away" announcements any more or less virtuous, but it did let*
> *me see it was a national effort.*

Received my first letter today. Was from Mother. "Good old Mom".

Saturday, July 21, 1945
Flew our first Pacific Mission today. Just a trg. mission and not an Empire strike.

Some Mission

I took my wind run and had a beautiful Ground speed and Drift. Just before turning on the I.P. we discover

BOMB BAY DOOR TROUBLE!

We went ahead—flew over the target and made a dry run. We then went around and again and on the next run we salvoed (*released our bombs simultaneously*). Later Jules (*the Bombardier*) had to crawl in the bomb bay and "kick" out the bombs that didn't go on salvo. (*A dangerous job to work in the open Bomb Bay thousands of feet above ground*).

Sunday, July 22, 1945
Toured the Island today. We hitchhiked all over. I believe we hiked more than we hitched. Saw a lot of the caves in which the Japs hid. Makes you realize how lucky you are to have a base like we have. Take my hat off to the Marines and Infantry.

> *Note: Some Japanese soldiers were "holdouts" until after the War ended. They had been taught never to surrender and many would commit suicide rather than give up. This was the*

basis for the "Kamikaze" suicide flyers. It was also the reason we were so grateful we never had to invade the Japanese home islands, because it was believed the entire population was being trained to fight to the death and not surrender—all of which made the book about our "Last Mission" (August 14-15) so intriguing.

Monday, July 23, 1945

Flew the Patoris mission today. Really had a good run. Bob estimated our bombs hit about 50-100' right. Not bad from 15,000'.

We went on up to Iwo. Looked at Mt. Suribachi. Strategically the island is important. But actually I bet it wouldn't draw $10 at an auction. To think thousands of men gave their lives for such a place is positively revolting. This so-called civilization is disgusting. If people would think a little more of God and a lot less of Gold we'd be much better off.

Note: When I landed later at Iwo Jima, I found it truly was the most desolate war scared area I ever encountered. It was total destruction. What I didn't realize at that time was that all those men sacrificed their lives so that those of us flying in the B-29s would have a place to land if we ran short on fuel—since Iwo Jima is closer to Japan than our bases on Guam, Tinian and Saipan. It makes me ashamed as I re-read this entry because I was so self-righteous and judgmental. In the intervening years I have found that life is often not totally black or white—much of the time we find we settle for the best shade of grey we can get—and pray for God's grace to sustain us.

Tuesday, July 24, 1945

Today was pretty much a "day of rest". We generally loafed around. Morale seems to be pretty high. The boys are bitching, naturally—but then it wouldn't be the army of they weren't! All in all they are doing a fine job.

Results on the raids have been very good. Hope they keep on this way. We had hopes of going on the next one but am afraid we won't get to. We can't fly Truk (*Island*) 'til next month. We are a little bitter because one of these days all hell is going to blow loose and I want to have in as many missions as possible before it does.

> *Note: I don't remember exactly what I thought was going to happen. Maybe we were looking forward to the anticipated invasion of Japan, which never came to pass because of the Atomic Bombs and Japan's surrender. That probably saved hundreds of thousands of lives!*

Thursday, July 26, 1945

The 502nd (*Bomb Group*) flew another raid—Lost a 402nd (*Squadron*) plane. Sure feel sorry for their wives and parents as I know how they will feel.

> *Note: As I mentioned before, my brother, Leon Martin, was killed in a B-24 air-crash over England a few months earlier (March, 1945). He left behind a wife, a small daughter and an unborn daughter who arrived a few months after his death. So many thousands sacrificed everything during those war years so we could have a free America in a freer world. We owe them far more than we can ever repay.*

Hope some of them got out O.K. Reports indicate they didn't tho.

We worked on the new area this afternoon. Spent part of the time working on the (*Officer's*) Club and part of it working on the 430th (*Squadron*) E. M. barracks.

Pretty good—can't detail E.M. to build Officer barracks but they can detail Officers to build E.M. barracks. Ha Ha.

Friday July 27, 1945

Put up a little life insurance today. Spent the afternoon at the ship cutting up "flak curtains" (*protection from shell bursts*) to put around my position. Put some on my seat. (Hate to get hit there & not be able to sit down) some to protect my head and back and some for my legs and some to put my feet on. With my flak suit and helmet I should be pretty well protected. Funny about one Flight Engineer. He was hit by a piece of flak that came through between the Navigator and Radio man. Lucky for them but not him.

Chapter 4

Air Raids On Tokyo, Ube, and Akita
August 1–15, 1945

Note: _Our B-29s were stripped down with only tail-guns so we could fly faster and further. We hoped the Japanese never realized we had no guns on the sides, belly, top or nose. We were painted black on the undercarriage to help us avoid detection when we flew over our targets (usually oil refineries) at night. Our usual routine was to leave late in the day, reach our target after midnight and return to Guam on the following morning. These were long flights, but the sunrises and sunsets over the Pacific Ocean were often spectacularly beautiful._

Raid # 1 Tokyo Refinery

Wednesday and Thursday, August 1 and 2, 1945
Well, today was the big day. Target Tokyo. Guess we were right when we guessed we would start flying missions about August 1ˢᵗ.

"Preflighted" our sets—then went to church. We were too late for services but "Chappie" (_The Chaplain_) gave us a special communion. Really helps to know that you are at peace with yourself and God.

Was a long mission going up. Seemed as if we would never arrive. At "begin climb" point we donned our oxygen masks (_in the event we were hit and lost pressure_) and "flak suits" (_to protect against shell bursts_). Really had a tough time getting into it. Must weigh 30 lbs.

Hit land fall on the nose. Made our wind runs. Turned to IP (*initial point of our bomb run*) then toward target. We sent one of the scanners to the camera hatch to throw out the "rope (*streamers to deflect search lights and guns*). He got his headset jerked off and didn't know his mike was on. Kept breathing into (*it*) very loudly.

The run on the target seems now as only a bad dream. I've never been so nervous or frightened in my life. Seemed as if everyone was shouting at once. Bev, "Throw out some more rope". Scanner, "I am, I am." I thought I'd go crazy. Then a bright (?) hit my window & the left side of the ship was thrown—Bob and I (we later talked about) both thought the "Big Hutch" was hit in #1 or #2.

When "bombs away" point came we broke away (*the pilots quickly turned us off the bomb run*). I was so scared I could hardly breath. From then on we had no trouble.

The scanners reported flak but since I had my window covered (had the light on) I couldn't see it. For Bob, Perk and I it was like being inside a sub with depth-charges going off around you.

> *Note:* We bombed in single file across the target. Later one of the pilots told me he counted the search lights shining on the plane ahead of us. He stopped when he got to about 60, (I think was the number) because it was too scary. These lights helped the enemy gunners on the ground train their guns on us, and the pilot knew we were next in line.

Got home with no trouble. I give my thanks to God—

Saturday, August 4, 1945.
Moved to the new area today. Worked hard building our new floor and putting up our 3 tents. Really proud of our "Little Home"—

Don't know when we will get into our Pre-Fabs—Hope it isn't too long. However, the way we are fixed now it isn't bad at all. Cool breeze blows thru most of the day and nite—

We go on another raid tomorrow. Won't say where. Should be a fairly easy mission—for my money there isn't an easy mission—3000 miles of nothing but water takes care of that—

Raid #2—Ube Refinery

Sunday and Monday, August 5 and 6, 1945
Sure was a long stretch—about 16 hours in the air. That is too long. Makes about 26-30 hrs on every mission with no "sack" time.

> *Note: We had to get briefed before each mission to get information about the target, etc. so we could make preparations. Each person then checked the plane and/or equipment he would utilize during the flight. Crew members physically pulled (in a circular arc) the propellers of each engine to prepare them to start. A little like pre-cranking an old automobile before the advent of the automatic starter. We took off from two runways at one minute intervals, putting one of our long line of planes into the air every 30 seconds. Upon our return we were debriefed to tell ground personnel what had happened. We usually got coffee and doughnuts from the Red Cross ladies when we returned. After that we were ready for the sack.*

As far as "flak" went we didn't see any—only a couple of searchlights and "probably" one night fighter.

Trip up was long but uneventful—except—the compass went out and threw us about 75 miles off course before we knew it. Caught it by a loran fix and altered back in.

Bob wasn't sure just where we were but I picked up the coast on the "Mickey" and identified our position. I altered into the "Landfall"—took a wind run, turned onto I.P. made another wind run—then a rate check on IP.—

About 20 mi from target the Mickey went out. I tried to fix it and couldn't. Gave the ship to "Julio" who made a couple of fires (*started by the bombs dropped by planes ahead of us*) his tg—about 10 miles out the set went on again. Since he changed his sightings for his run I let him keep it & just made sure he was on the right target.

On the way in we almost collided with another ship—Johnny "yanked" us up 300 feet and almost "stalled" we went up so fast. Sure is hard to see others up there at nite.

> <u>Note</u>: *Because of the nature of our new radar equipment and because we were engaging in night flights, we flew single ship missions rather than the traditional formations used by other groups. It had many advantages, but it also had additional dangers from unexpectedly getting too close to other planes which were flying the same bomb run. In addition, it could be rather lonely flying over thousands of miles of ocean.*

We thought we had a nite fighter but if we did we "shook" him.

Gas ran awfully low. On "final" after reaching the base we had an induction fire in #1 (*engine*). #3 was backfiring & #4 smoking badly. It really had us sweating awhile. We all had our "chutes" on & the hatch clear to jump.

Landed O.K. tho with all four (*engines*) running. Hubba-Hubba

Tuesday August 7, 1945
Heard today that the new atomic bomb had been tested on Japan. Debris was sighted up to 45,000 feet. 16 miles were said to be destroyed. Equivalent to destroying power of 1000 B 29's. Certainly hope this ends the war. I hate to think what another one would be like if both sides were able to manufacture the explosive. God help us all.

Thursday, August 9, 1945
The boys had another raid tonite. Amagasaki Oil Works at Osaka!—

We had been told that the mission was cancelled so I went on sick call. (*I was having fungus in my ear*). The result was that I was put on DNIF (*non flying status*). That was O.K until we discovered (at a birthday party for Bob's new little boy, Larry) that plans had been changed.

I stood by and waved goodbye to the guys as they left. Sure is a funny feeling when you know you may be the only one of the crew alive the next time. I (and Bob, too) seemed to have an awful foreboding about the flight. As it happened they did have to feather (*shut down*) #2 (*engine*). You'll never understand how I felt there waiting to hear if they were safe or in the Pacific. They planned to land at Iwo, then Saipan but since they had enough gas they came on in—

Today (Friday, August 10, 1945)

I am 20—Today I yam a man—Ha Ha—I (*one*) year and I can vote. Hubba Hubba

Saturday, August 11, 1945
BOY—WHAT A SURPISE

I was awakened last nite by everything from submachine guns &.45's to the town criers who informed us THE WAR WAS OVER! Naturally we didn't know what to think.

First thing this morning we checked the bulletin boards & kept an ear to the radio. An announcer told us nothing would be said til morn which is tonite here. I pray to God it is over.

Sunday, August 12, 1945
Everyone is going around in circles today. Is it *is* or is it *isn't*!? Don't think we wouldn't like to know!

The mission for tonite has been put off 'til tomorrow nite. We don't know yet where it will be if we make it. Bets are going Hi wide and handsome—Both ways! But everyone hopes and prayers are being turned to only one direction! We are all hoping, yet afraid to hope too hard 'lest our illusion be shattered and our morale with it! For if we lose our morale it would make it hell on earth here. I pray it is peace & victory—if not—we will continue as we had planned!

Monday, August 13, 1945
No news may be good news but it is certainly hard to wait for it. I am just getting a taste of what the folks at home have been going thru for 3 yrs. I would rather fly another mission than this!- ! We have been hearing rumors all day long—It is—It isn't—etc, etc, etc, ! ———

They can't hope to hold out much longer and look at the lives that will be saved if we have peace now. The atomic bomb is enough in itself to make them want peace—But that, coupled with Russia's entry into the war—well – !!!—It seems more than they can stand.

"The Last Mission"

Raid #3 Akita Refinery

Tuesday and Wednesday, August 14 and 15, 1945
Well the war is on again. At least for us! The General Staff must have gotten tired of waiting—they waited once before while signing a peace pact with Japan and got stabbed in the back for their trouble. This time—when the paper is signed—then we quit fighting.

> *Note: The Japanese fleet was secretly sailing across the Pacific to bomb Pearl Harbor on December 7, 1941, at the same time their diplomats were negotiating with our Government in Washington, D.C. President Roosevelt described their surprise attack as a "day that will live in Infamy".*

Tonite is <u>the</u> nite.

We go on the longest bombing range ever conceived by man. Nearly 4000 miles non stop carrying 52 250# bombs and only 6785 gals of gas.

> *Note: Later, I realized this was about the same distance as flying from Wichita to Seattle and return, in our 1945 propeller driven airplanes—without refueling.*

We left here at 0825 Z (1825 K) for Akita—the northern most part of Japan (Honshu) to be attacked by B-29s. Before leaving we were told by Col Seymore the war was over. However things weren't all settled and no orders had come in cancelling the strike. Utah was to be the call sign and we were assured we wouldn't go beyond Iwo. (Except for 3000 miles we didn't)

> *Note: At first they said we wouldn't get past briefing. Next they told us to get in our planes but we probably wouldn't get off the runway. Then it was to the target. Finally, we got the good news on the way back.*

Had no trouble over the Empire. Picked up land corrected into L.F. From there to I.P. then to TG. The smoke was so dense and bad (we were at 11,000' & the smoke went well over our heads) that Bev almost turned off before we reached the target. Instead we flew into and didn't know if we would get out, the thermals were so bad.

Coming home we heard the Big News—after 3/12 years—the WAR IS FINALLY OVER! THANK GOD!

We really "sweat it out", too. 1, 2 & 3 were all backfiring & we didn't know if our gas would last or not.

When we arrived they told us there would be a party—AND WHAT A PARTY! Never has there been such a party. Ha-Ha-

Note: The 315th Bomb Wing received a Presidential Unit Citation for its work in "radar bombing" Japan. The orders for our 502nd Bomb Group read in part as follows:

"The 502nd Bombardment Group (VH) is cited for outstanding performance of duty in action against the enemy. During the period from 5 August 1945 to 15 August 1945, this organization struck crippling blows at the Japanese petroleum industry. The action demonstrated the high efficiency, courage and resolution of 502nd personnel and characterized the spirit of air attack throughout the war. Particularly was this true in view of the fact that this organization employed recently developed radar bombing instrument and it flew B-29 aircraft which had been stripped of all defensive armament except three .50 caliber tail machine guns. On the night of 5 August, 1945 the 502nd Bombardment Group (VH) attacked the Ube Coal Liquefaction plant at Ube, an important producer of synthetic oil. This installation was of major importance to the Japanese war effort as the enemy had been virtually cut off by naval blockade to sources of crude oil.....On the night of 14 August, 1945 the 502nd Bombardment Group (VH) attacked the Nippon Oil Refinery at Tsuchizaki, an important petroleum installation which had heretofore been considered inaccessible because of it great distance from any allied air base. This mission of 3,740 statute miles was flown non-stop without bomb bay tanks. Despite the great distance, this group carried a bomb load which had previously been considered large for missions of shorter range. Braving the dangers of a long overwater flight without the protection of friendly fighters, the aircrews attacked the target and left it a smoking ruin. Later reconnaissance revealed that every part of the installation had been hit by bombs and that the refinery was almost completely destroyed or damaged. Despite fatigue, the hazards of long over-water flights in adverse weather conditions, and the threat of enemy attacks, flying personnel of this organization demonstrated at all times a willingness to perform their duties at peak efficiency. Matching the aircrews in accomplishment were the ground personnel, who showed meritorious initiative, perseverance and fidelity in carrying out their assignments, working long hours with incomplete facilities. The achievements of the 502nd Bombardment Group (VH) during this period contributed greatly to the destruction of the major oil refining and storage capacity of Japan and drastically reduced the power and ability of the enemy to continue the war, thereby bring great honor to the United States Army Air Forces and to the entire military service"

Over 50 years later, I read a new book entitled, "The Last Mission", by Jim Smith and Malcolm McConnell. They discussed the Akita raid in detail, and advanced the theory that our flight unknowingly stopped a coup by some of the

Japanese military who were attempting to capture the Imperial Palace and the Emperor and keep the war going. When our planes went by Tokyo, the Japanese government "blacked out" the city and the Emperor's palace, and apparently thwarted the rebels' plans. This all showed me that God may be doing something through us of which we are not aware. In our case, it arguably meant saving thousands of military and civilians from being killed if the war had continued. We need to plan and act, but the final results are still in God's hands. As Proverbs 16:9 says:

"In his heart a man plans his course,
but the LORD determines his steps."

The book was later made into a documentary movie by the History Channel. I am deeply grateful to the authors for all their work in researching and recording the operation of our B-29s and particularly about this "Last Mission". It has been a priceless bit of history to pass on to our family.

Chapter 5

Awaiting a Formal Surrender
August 16–23, 1945

Thursday, August 16, 1945
Well, it was a good party as far as we were concerned—However – the Col didn't (*agree*)—We G.I.ed the mess hall today and were told there would be no drinking 'til 21st noon and we're all confined to Base 'til 19th noon!

Friday, August 17, 1945
We finally started our "Pre Fab" today. The Col. told us the tents would come down 21st at noon—Soooooo—we decided we'd better get started—

We got the floor and most of the sides done.

The war seems to be over. But—they haven't signed that little piece of paper. Til they do we can't be sure—even then we can't after the "deal" they pulled last time.

Saturday, August 18, 1945
Still working on the Pre-Fab—should finish it tomorrow—we hope.

They still haven't signed that Paper!!! Sure will be glad when they do. So will millions of others. BET THE PEOPLE AT HOME ARE REALLY HAVING A "HEY-DAY"————

Sunday, August 19, 1945
Still working on the Pre-Fab. Had it ready to move into by tonite, tho.

"Chappie" really preached a good sermon—told us it was high time that he quit telling us what a hard lot we had & patting us on the back. Instead—he proceeded to tell us how we (& he included himself) had slipped from our prewar standards— really made the boys sit up & think!—When he asked for those who wanted to stay and rededicate themselves, to do so—about 30 stayed.

Monday, August 20, 1945
Finally moved into our new home—built myself a desk—shoe rack, and a place to hang my clothes and also one to hang my towels—

WE HAD CHOCOLATE CAKE ALA-MODE—WHOOPEE—IT REALLY TASTED GOOD!—

Funny how much little things mean when you don't have them. Sure will seem swell to be able to go in and order what you want and have it brought to you—Hubba Hubba_____

I understand the Jap delegation is at Manila—Everything is going fine!

Tuesday, August 21, 1945
Haven't heard any new news!

Understand we will have classes in Spanish, French, Math, etc. unless we go home within a month.

Naturally the rumors are flying thick and fast. Everyone has a new rumor.

Hope we get home by Christmas!

Chapter 6

Flight To The Philippines
August 24-September 1, 1945

Wednesday, August 22, 1945

13 crews went to Florida Blanca, Luzon—going to pick up parachutes (cargo).

Charlie's crew went but he didn't want to go. Said it was just 3000 more miles of ocean and he didn't want to stick his neck out. In a way he is right but I wouldn't have missed the chance. Being this close I would have gone.

Friday, August 24, 1945

Made another tour of the island today. Got a lot of pictures. Hope they turn out O.K. Got a lot of pictures of ox carts, scenery, etc.

When we got back at the field we found out we were going to Manila. One crew was back. They did get to Manila but said inflation was bad and the city was almost completely destroyed.

We are leaving at 0200 in the morning.

Saturday, August 25, 1945

Got off the ground at 0230 K. Trip up was a rough one. We hit some bad up-drafts in the thunderstorms. Lighting was bad. We even had St Elmo's fire (*colorful electric display*) on the nose. The weather continued for nearly 150 miles.

When we finally got to Luzon we circled over Manila, Bataan and Corregidor. I got some good pictures of all of them. Also a lot of pictures of the ships in the harbor. There were several hundred ships.

Sunday, August 26, 1945
Went into Manila via the A.T.C. shuttle plane. I saw an acquaintance from Boca Raton on the plane and flew on up to Clark Field with him. Just an air strip like any other.

> _Note:_ _Because of its importance during the early days of the war when the Philippines were being over-run by the Japanese, Clark Field had taken on an almost legendary status. Reality has a way of puncturing legends._

Jules and I then went on in to Manila. Got a ride into town. Got a lot of good pictures. Town is almost completely demolished. Will take a decade to rebuild, the civilians estimate.

It is just one big curio shop and bar. Inflation was bad—

1 peso (50c) for a coke.

> _Note:_ _We were used to paying 5c for a coke in the States!_

Took us from 7:30 p.m. til 1:30 a.m. to return—hitchhiking–

> _Note:_ _I have no idea why I reverted to "p.m." and "a.m." time. Perhaps I was emphasizing that hitchhiking for 6 hours across a strange Island at night wasn't the smartest thing in the world._

Met several Filipino soldiers on the way home. Had fun seeing how much of their language I could understand. They have a queer mixture of Spanish, Filipino and English.

We got a steak for 4 pesos (which was cheap) that was good. The food in general—at the Base and civilian is very poor. Was a pleasure to get back to Guam.

Thursday, August 30, 1945
Bill ditched, it is reported. No word has been heard since he left the Philippines. That makes 4 from the Group. One lost last week who crashed into a mt. on Saipan. One shot down over Tokyo. One crashed (blew up) just after he took off. We're losing more men off these cargo hauls than we lost in combat.

Sure did hate to see Bill get it. He was a right guy. One of the best pilots in the outfit!

Saturday, September 1, 1945
Several crews went out early to search for Bill's plane. They have no idea where he went down so they'll have to search all 1500 miles. They claim that the sea was so high no one could live in it over a few minutes.

They did discover an empty life raft. It was about 600 miles out and 30 mi left of course. They say surface winds must have been 60 mph or better. That tropical storm evidently turned into a typhoon—which spells trouble. All flights are canceled to Manila 'til further notice!_____

Chapter 7

Training for Parachute Jumps at Sea
September 7, 1945

"O-HO—for the life of a sailor– !

We put out to sea again today—Bearded skipper and all. (*The ship captain had a beard—unusual for us.*) Really had quite a good time.

We went out in an LCI (*Landing Craft Infantry*) from a small cove on the other side of the island—Very beautiful spot by the way.—

We practiced dropping from a 20' perch with parachute and Mae West.

> *Note: When we flew we were equipped with survival gear, parachute and an inflatable life preserver named after a popular actress of the 1930's. To avoid injury we learned to wait until we were in the water to inflate our Mae West.*

When we finished we all went for a swim. It was really nice. Had the gunners mate "topside" with a rifle & knife to take care of any sharks we might see. (We were informed they had gotten 7 the time before but we didn't see any—Praise be).

> <u>*Note:*</u> *We were never sure whether this was a "fish story" for our benefit or not—but seeing him sitting there with a rifle sure did get our attention!*

It was so smooth and pleasant everyone had a fine time—No sea sickness. Ha Ha

Coming home wasn't so good tho. We ran into a rain storm & were actually cold for awhile!

Glad to get back!

Chapter 8

<u>Promotions</u>
September 8, 1945

"The gold has turned to silver"—

In other words—I got promoted today—along with about 1000 others. Ha Ha. Johnny, Jules & Bob all got theirs.

> <u>Note:</u> *2ⁿᵈ Lt "bars" were "gold", and 1ˢᵗ Lt. "bars" were "silver". It sounds backward—but there probably is a tradition someplace in history that got it started that way.*

We had to report to the "Old Man" (*our Commanding Officer*) for them. Those he thought did something wrong in saluting He made read the IDR—(*Military regulations*)

No one is happy for they are afraid they will have to stay over longer. Because it will make the points higher.

> <u>Note:</u> *Perhaps it took more points for higher rated people to be eligible to return home. I don't remember. The years seem to erase some memories—and enlarge others!*

However, I have so few I'll be last anyway—Hubba Hubba.

Note: *A popular song of that era said:*

> *"Bless 'em all, Bless 'em all*
> *The long and the short and the tall,*
> *There'll be no promotion, this side of the ocean*
> *So cheer up my lads, Bless 'em all!"*

The rhyme turned out to be true for a lot of us.

Chapter 9

Flight to Hokkaido, Japan
September 13–17, 1945

Thursday, September 13, 1945

Learned late this evening that we might take an RON (*Remain Over Night*) trip to Japan. Don't know where yet! Sure hope we get it. —Later—

Went to briefing about 2300. Really a hurry up job. They want several communication men and interpreters as well as some communication supplies to be flown to Chitose (Hokkaido) just above Honshu! There will be 13 ships make the mission. The idea is to get the materiel there for Gen's Doolittle and Lemay when they make their nonstop trip from Hokkaido to Washington D.C.

Friday, September 14, 1945

Took off about 0400 this morning. The weather was P.P. Ceiling about 400' with rain and mist. Visibility was way down.

Flew to Iwo, refueled and took off for Hokkaido! Made G.S. up to 300 mph. Arrived about 1500 only to find it "socked in"—I brought us down using AB altimeter but didn't trust the map and the scope to go in blind as the maps aren't too good of that area and the scope was acting up.

Returned by way of Tokyo. The town is razed to the ground. Saw our TG at Kawasaki! We did a good job.

237

Landed Iwo about 2130. Try again tomorrow.

> *Note: Trips like this excited me then. Now it makes me tired!*

Saturday, September 15, 1945

Got up about 0600 but didn't get off the ground til 1100. Engine trouble. No trouble going up. Bad weather had cleared. No trouble landing.

I stepped out of the plane and ran into Dale McCoy. Boy ! Was I surprised & he too.

> *Note: Dale and I, together with several others from Wichita, left for active duty shortly after High School. We both went to Navigation School and ended up in the Pacific theater. After the war our experience at Hokkaido gave us a special life long "talking point" whenever we met.*

Japs were swarming all around the plane. All soldiers and bowing, saluting and smiling.

Dale came over in a truck from Chitose N.A.F. to Chitose AAF to where I was. Spent the nite with him under the wing of their C 46. Used Jap blankets (after using an aerosol bomb to delouse them.)

> *Note: As we went across the now dark airfield in an old truck with Japanese all around, I wondered if it was very smart with only a .45 caliber pistol. We were told the Academy where we were going was to train men for Kamikaze (suicide) missions. The Japanese had not yet disbanded and they were still operational.*

We had a Japanese interpreter who said he came from the USA to Japan in the early 1930's to receive an estate and they drafted him. He had been in Manchuria and was now here in Chitose. The interpreter told us we could sleep inside the Academy, but we said, "No Thanks!" He brought blankets and pillows (which were quite hard and felt like sacks filled with rice husks instead of feathers). He also told us that he would have a Japanese soldier wake us, but he wouldn't get close to us. Sure enough, we were awakened the next day by a man peeking at us around the end of the plane, but he kept his distance and left as soon as we were up.

Sunday, September 16, 1945

Boy! Was it cold last nite. Used 4 blankets and still I like to froze. Got up 0500—went in to Academy to eat—All food 10 in 1 rations (*Pre packaged food supplied by U.S.*).

About 0630 the P.W.s (*Allied Prisoners of War*) arrived that were being ferried out in the C 46's. Never saw any group of people so happy. Said they had gained 30 lbs/man in 4 wks on the supplies we (*U.S. planes*) flew in. There were English, Dutch, Aussies & Yanks—From Singapore, Malay, Bataan, Wake, etc. We were the first Americans they had seen in 3-4 yrs.

Got lots of pictures and souvenirs from the Japs—a bill for my short snorter (*Paper money from various places we pasted together to form a long roll of bills*). I forgot to get pictures of the Jap formations at the Academy. Should also have gotten a picture of me trying to convey by sign language that I had left a bag in the truck. Ha Ha.

Had to leave before noon. No trouble going back to Iwo. Stayed all nite. Got up 0430 & came back—I navigated from Iwo to here (*Guam*).

Arrived about 1030 and learned there was rumor we were missing—We quickly fixed that. You should hear the wild tales about the trip the E.M. are spreading—Geisha girls on down.

Chapter 10

An "Almost" Flight to the United States
October 1–10, 1945

Monday, October 1, 1945

Another day—another dollar. Another month— another $250.
(*My monthly pay, including a premium for "flight pay"*)

This has been quite a day. I was informed I was to be Squadron Supply Officer—the worst job in the Army—Sure wish I could get out of it. But looks like I am stuck!

> *Note: All army equipment had to be accounted for, including planes. A rumor went around when we arrived at Guam that we had an extra ship with no paper work. Probably just a joke but at least that was better than having paper work and no ship! It was this kind of problem that concerned me, on a much smaller scale, when they made me Supply Officer.*

Good news, too, tho!!–!!–!!

Looks like low point man Martin (36 with 2 battle stars) is getting something good out of having the fewest pts besides Squadron Supply. Maj. Ross told me I had been selected as Radar man on a crew to fly some General back to the states from the Philippines. Hubba Hubba—We were to leave tomorrow, but has been postponed indefinitely! Sure hope it pulls thru– !

241

Wednesday, October 10, 1945

It looks as if our mission is off. Nothing more has been said. Sooooo—Too bad—Martin—T.S.

Chapter 11

Some Planes Leave for the United States
November 24, 1945

Today was a Big Day for some of the fellows. The Sunset Project is getting underway (15 planes for our Group) and 6 are leaving today. Charlie and Bob are both on board.

Took a lot of pictures and sent them home on Charlie's plane. They should be in the states by Tuesday.

Bob's leaving left Al the only man on his crew left. Guess we will have to get together for bridge.

This is the first excitement we've had for two months or more.

Note: Many months would go by before I made another entry in the Diary. Someone once described "flying" as "hours and hours of utter boredom, punctuated by moments of stark terror"! In some ways those days on Guam after the war fit that description. Long periods of little excitement, and then a flight would come along that could really get our attention!

Actually we had a lot of fun. We passed the time in many enjoyable ways. Lots of card games. Some athletics. Some of the time we spent in classes. At one point we got the parachute department to make us a sail, and put it on a boat we bought from someone so we could sail in beautiful Tumon Bay. I have heard that in the years since the war that Guam, with its warm climate and some good beaches, has become a tourist attraction—for the Japanese and others. I suppose we had a wonderful thing going for us—but we just wanted to go home.

Chapter 12

Search Mission near Okinawa
March 21–22, 1946

Thursday, March 21, 1946

Left for Okinawa on a search mission today. A General is lost somewhere around Formosa (*now known as Taiwan*) in a B-17.

We typed up all the clearances last nite and then early this morning (0530 to be exact) Sullivan came in told me I was going to have to take the place of a Mickey man who didn't show up. They gave me 15 minutes to get packed for a two week trip.

Our search area was right along the coast of Formosa and we had to get down to 650' to get below the clouds. I kept the radar on all the time as I didn't want to run into any of the mountains as they go up to 14,000'. We finally had to give it up because of bad visibility and low ceiling. We were afraid we would be in the "drink" ourselves if we didn't.

As we started to leave the area and climb above the soup, engines # 1 and 2 backfired and you should have seen me start for my life raft. Ha Ha

Got back to Okinawa O.K and started to land. It was the "flyenest" air plane I have ever seen. It just didn't want to come down. We had to pull up the gear and go around. On the 2nd attempt we clocked 140 when we hit the runway and it should have been about 100 to 105. He finally managed to set it on the ground and make it stay.

About this time I heard over UHF (*Ultra high frequency radio*) that the general had been found. Ironically, he had cracked into the side of a mountain on Formosa and we had all been briefed explicitly not to fly over Formosa—

Friday, March 22, 1946
We had to sleep in a tent and during the night and I began to appreciate the weather on Guam. They only gave us one blanket and we all slept in our flying clothes. And were still frozen.

Took off about 0930 and flew back without incident. Got in 15:30 on the flight making a total of 23:30 (*hours of flight time*) for this month—That is the most since Hokkaido.

One thing I saw up there that interested me was the tombs. On nearly every hillside they had built some. I was certainly sorry I couldn't get a picture of some.

> *Note: We flew search missions in Florida and the Pacific. In addition, we spent many hours out over thousands of empty miles of ocean without seeing anything. It became pretty obvious to us that we were probably not going to be found if we ever had to ditch or bail out.*

Chapter 13

Many Crews Leave for the United States
March 24, 1946

Today was the Big Day for 442 Air Crew members as the first surplus bunch left for the states. It left me the last man on my crew to be here. All the rest of the ground crew and air crew are gone now. If I hadn't been grounded on that one mission I would have gotten my Air Medal and those 5 extra points would have put me on the list to go home.

However, I might have run into trouble on that mission so all in all I can't kick. Have no idea when I will leave, tho—Hope it is soon.

Chapter 14

Home to the United States
May 26–June 19, 1946

Monday, May 26, 1946
Found out I could go home, today & wired the folks to send confirmation.

Have been eligible since Feb 26, '46.

> *Note: Because my brother, Leon, had been killed, I became eligible to return home regardless of my point status. I didn't become aware of these orders until May 26. We worked through the Red Cross to get all the paper work completed.*

Sure will seem good to get back—

Have learned not to believe it til I see it. This will make my 3rd try—

Monday, June 10, 1946
Today I left Guam

(That is enough for the whole page)

Tuesday, June 11, 1946   Hawaii—
Landed here and our priority stopped with us. Won't get out 'til about Saturday. The Army is having a world wide "nose count" to see who and how many they have.

Note: It took about a year (or more) to bring millions of service men and women home from overseas. It must have been a huge logistical problem!

Sunday, June 16, 1946
ARRIVED STATESIDE WHOOPEE

Monday, June 17, 1946
Arrived Separation Center in San Francisco.

Wednesday, June 19, 1946

1100 (*a.m.*)

Today I am a free man. With this page I end my Army career—

I wouldn't part with it for a million dollars & I wouldn't go thru it again for another million.__.

**

I visited my brother, Claude, and his wife Shirley in Seattle, Washington, and then traveled by train to Wichita. I arrived home on July 4, 1945—My "Independence Day"!

ONE FINAL COMMENT

As I re-read the accounts I entered in the Diary over 60 years ago, I told Grandma Ellie I wondered if it all really happened. I do know that "'war stories' are more fun than 'wars'". Jesus said there would be "wars and rumors of wars" until His return. I believe Him. In the intervening years since WWII we have had the Korean War, the Cold War, the Viet Nam War, the Wars in Granada and Panama, the Gulf War, The War against Terrorism, The Iraq War and the War in Afghanistan, together with numerous other conflicts in or with country after country around the globe.

Few generations escape the awful blight and curse of War. I pray that each generation will know how to handle the crises when they occur in their lifetime, and that we will all realize the only real peace will come from following Jesus Christ and living eternally with Him in His Kingdom!

In the final analysis, the "time for war" spoken of in Ecclesiastes, is here on earth, and the "time for peace" (permanently) will come when those who are following Jesus join together in Heaven with Him and one another.

Grandma and I look forward to seeing you there.

From Grandpa With Love

Made in the USA
Charleston, SC
22 December 2016